Marketing Continuing Education

Hal Beder, *Editor*
Rutgers University

NEW DIRECTIONS FOR CONTINUING EDUCATION
GORDON G. DARKENWALD, *Editor-in-Chief*
Rutgers University
ALAN B. KNOX, *Consulting Editor*
University of Wisconsin

Number 31, Fall 1986

Paperback sourcebooks in
The Jossey-Bass Higher Education Series

Jossey-Bass Inc., Publishers
San Francisco • London

Hal Beder (Ed.).
Marketing Continuing Education.
New Directions for Continuing Education, no. 31.
San Francisco: Jossey-Bass, 1986.

New Directions for Continuing Education
Gordon G. Darkenwald, *Editor-in-Chief*
Alan B. Knox, *Consulting Editor*

New Directions for Continuing Education (publication number
USPS 493-930) is published quarterly by Jossey-Bass Inc., Publishers.
Second-class postage paid at San Francisco, California,
and at additional mailing offices. POSTMASTER: Send address
changes to Jossey-Bass Inc., Publishers, 433 California Street, San
Francisco, California 94104.

Editorial correspondence should be sent to the Editor-in-Chief,
Gordon G. Darkenwald, Graduate School of Education, Rutgers
University, 10 Seminary Place, New Brunswick, New Jersey 08903.

Library of Congress Catalog Card Number LC 85-81884

International Standard Serial Number ISSN 0195-2242

International Standard Book Number ISBN 1-55542-982-3

Cover art by WILLI BAUM

Ordering Information

The paperback sourcebooks listed below are published quarterly and can be ordered either by subscription or single-copy.

Subscriptions cost $40.00 per year for institutions, agencies, and libraries. Individuals can subscribe at the special rate of $30.00 per year *if payment is by personal check.* (Note that the full rate of $40.00 applies if payment is by institutional check, even if the subscription is designated for an individual.) Standing orders are accepted.

Single copies are available at $9.95 when payment accompanies order, and *all single-copy orders under $25.00 must include payment.* (California, New Jersey, New York, and Washington, D.C., residents please include appropriate sales tax.) For billed orders, cost per copy is $9.95 plus postage and handling. (Prices subject to change without notice.)

Bulk orders (ten or more copies) of any individual sourcebook are available at the following discounted prices: 10–49 copies, $8.95 each; 50–100 copies, $7.96 each; over 100 copies, *inquire.* Sales tax and postage and handling charges apply as for single copy orders.

Please note that these prices are for the academic year 1986–1987 and are subject to change without prior notice. Also, some titles may be out of print and therefore not available for sale.

To ensure correct and prompt delivery, all orders must give either the *name of an individual* or an *official purchase order number.* Please submit your order as follows:

Subscriptions: specify series and year subscription is to begin.
Single Copies: specify sourcebook code (such as, CE1) and first two words of title.

Mail orders for United States and Possessions, Latin America, Canada, Japan, Australia, and New Zealand to:
Jossey-Bass Inc., Publishers
433 California Street
San Francisco, California 94104

Mail orders for all other parts of the world to:
Jossey-Bass Limited
28 Banner Street
London EC1Y 8QE

New Directions for Continuing Education
Gordon G. Darkenwald, *Editor-in-Chief*
Alan B. Knox, *Consulting Editor*

Contents

Editor's Notes

In recent years, continuing education has been characterized by several important changes. Continuing education activity has grown dramatically, especially in industry, the professions, and government. Continuing education units have increasingly been required to finance their own operations through fee income, and an increase in the number of providers has interjected competition as a major factor to be dealt with. Furthermore, with the advent of the "knowledge explosion," the environment in which continuing education operates has become exceptionally dynamic. Given these realities, if continuing education units are to be successful, they can no longer be managed on an ad hoc basis. They must operate according to a planned strategy that takes into account the influences of the environment and results in an enhanced ability to attract learners. Marketing is fundamental to such a strategy.

The purpose of this sourcebook is to explain the marketing concept and to describe some of the methods associated with marketing. In the first chapter, Beder begins with an explanation and discussion of basic marketing principles, the most important being the notion of exchange. Subsequent chapters by Smith, Willard and Warren, Falk, Fischer, and Mason discuss tools and methods that derive from basic principles, and which are embodied in what are commonly called the four P's—product, promotion, place, and price. Martel and Colley, in an important shift in direction, then follow with an examination of ethical issues raised by the marketing approach.

There is a major thread woven throughout this sourcebook that merits mention at the outset. Marketing, as we use the term here, is a strategy, as distinct from a tactic. As such, it must be planned, must operate at all program levels, must be continuously assessed, and must be modified as experience and evaluative information dictates.

Hal Beder
Editor

*Hal Beder is associate professor of adult and continuing
education at Rutgers University and directs the continuing
education program of the Rutgers Graduate School of
Education. A former editor of* Adult Education Quarterly, *
he also edited the New Directions sourcebook*
Realizing the Potential of Interorganizational Cooperation.
He received his doctorate from Columbia University.

Understanding of basic concepts and principles is essential to
formulating an effective marketing strategy.

Basic Concepts and Principles of Marketing

Hal Beder

It is appropriate to begin this volume on marketing with a definition of
its central topic. Rados (1981) defines marketing as follows: "Marketing . . . deals with the many methods by which A tries to get B to do his
will, where B has the freedom to act as he chooses" (p. 17). Although this
definition is rather broad, in considering it, the value of marketing for
continuing education becomes clear. Adults, by virtue of their adult status,
control their own lives. In Rados' terms, they have the freedom to act as
they choose. Since adult learners generally participate in continuing education on their own volition, continuing educators need methods to attract
learners to their offerings. Given that there is considerable competition for
adults' time and money from other life activities, as well as from other
providers of education, a methodology for attracting them is all the more
important if continuing education programs are to have sufficient
numbers of learners.

Marketing is, among other things, a methodology for attracting
learners, a methodology that guides program development, promotion,
pricing, distribution, and market research, all of which will be discussed
in detail in this volume. Yet marketing is more than a mere methodology.
It is also a body of theory regarding consumer decision making that bor-
rows extensively from all the social sciences. This is important for at least

H. Beder (Ed.). *Marketing Continuing Education.*
New Directions for Continuing Education, no. 31. San Francisco: Jossey-Bass, Fall 1986.

two reasons. First, as with all theories, the components of marketing are interrelated and integrated. Consequently, a marketing orientation can provide an excellent overarching perspective that can guide and coordinate most of the activities of program development and delivery, activities that might otherwise be treated as being disparate and unconnected. Second, because of its solid basis in social science research and success in practice, marketing has both theoretical and practical validity; or, to put it more simply, it works.

What, then, is marketing all about? Perhaps Kotler (1975) provides the most useful definition: "Marketing is the analysis, planning, implementation, and control of carefully formulated programs designed to bring about voluntary exchanges of values with target markets for the purpose of achieving organizational objectives. It relies heavily on designing the organization's offering in terms of target markets' needs and desires and on using effective pricing, communication, and distribution to inform, motivate and service the markets" (p. 5).

Organizational Objectives

As defined, marketing is a strategy for accomplishing organizational objectives, and if marketing is to achieve this end, it is critical that continuing educators have a clear understanding of their organizations' missions. Clarity of mission is important because lack of clarity may have two unfortunate consequences. First, programs developed will lack coherence and participation, and income will suffer. Second, and ultimately more important, the continuing education unit will soon find itself at odds with its parent institution as it develops programs that conflict with the larger institution's philosophy. In power struggles that develop over conflicts of mission, continuing education seldom wins.

For marketing to be successful, it must be applied strategically at all levels of program operation. The past history of successes and failures must be considered in respect to the present in developing marketing plans for the future. Likewise, market strategy must be orchestrated at the unit level and applied at the individual program level. Failure to apply a planned and holistic approach to marketing greatly reduces its effectiveness.

Exchange

Given that marketing begins with a clear understanding of and solid commitment to organizational objectives, what must follow is a clear understanding of the mechanism that makes it work, the mechanism of exchange. The concept of exchange lies at the core of the marketing approach and gives meaning to all the techniques that follow.

The basic objective of marketing is to establish the conditions whereby a learner is willing to exchange resources he or she values to acquire something valued more—continuing education offerings. Exchange is reciprocal. From the continuing educator's perspective, time and effort are expended to develop valued programs in return for learners' fee income and the ability to achieve educational objectives. The process works most effectively when both provider and learner are benefiting the most with the least expenditure of resources.

From a practical standpoint, it is necessary to know at least two things before the exchange process can be managed for mutual benefit. First, we must know what things learners value and how much they value them. Second, we must understand the costs learners incur—the resources they must relinquish to participate.

Value

Let us first consider the issue of value. Very useful tools in analyzing value are the concepts of tangible and core product, concepts we shall return to later on. The tangible product is the product we see and touch. In the case of continuing education, it is the physical manifestation of instructors, location, materials, and so forth. The core product is the essential benefit the learner expects to derive from participation. For example, the core product for a business executive taking a course in gardening may be recreation and perhaps escape from the pressures of daily work. The core product for a retiree taking a course in cabinetmaking might be maintaining a positive self-image through continued productivity. The concept of core product is critical because, generally speaking, the core product underlies motivation to participate.

Essential benefits that represent the value of continuing education to learners may be classified as being either instrumental or expressive. Instrumental benefits are benefits that are direct means to some other end. A literacy student, for example, may be enrolled in high school equivalency to obtain a desired diploma, with the expectation of then securing a better job. A recent law graduate might be enrolled in a preparation course to pass the bar exam and then practice law. Frequently, instrumental benefits have direct economic consequences for learners, and the decision to participate represents a conscious economic investment on their part. For example, it is quite likely that a beginning lawyer would be willing to invest a significant amount of his or her personal resources in a bar exam preparation course, in the expectation that the resources gained after passing the exam would far outweigh the costs of the course.

When learners perceive that substantial instrumental benefits will result from participation, and when they can estimate the return on their investments, it is relatively easy to predict whether they will exchange.

The case is less simple when expressive benefits are at stake. Expressive benefits are the feelings of pleasure or gratification that result from the act of participation itself or from the learning gained during participation. For example, the benefit derived from participation in a "great books" study group is intellectual stimulation, and the benefit to a housewife participating in a course in wildlife photography may be escape from daily routine. Expressive benefits are important to consider, since they are frequently as important in motivation as instrumental benefits are.

Although the extent of perceived benefit is important to an understanding of why learners participate, it is only half of the equation. Equally important is an understanding of the costs of participation. Costs go well beyond fees, although fees can be a major part of the resources the learner exchanges for service. As important, and sometimes more important, are the opportunity costs involved. Opportunity costs represent the value of all the things that must be forgone so that the learner can participate. Most significant is the time that could be spent doing other things. Sometimes time can be assessed in purely economic terms. For example, if real estate brokers are asked whether they support mandatory continuing education for relicensure, many may say no; their reasoning might be that although knowledge of the finer points of real estate would be valuable for the agents who work for them, they are most concerned with one thing—sales, and every hour spent in education is an hour not spent on income-producing sales. The opportunity costs are simply too high.

Although in this example opportunity costs are patently economic, this is not always the case. Adults, because they must successfully perform a multiplicity of roles, incur a multiplicity of responsibilities. When participation in continuing education necessitates time away from the family or the job, or even when it conflicts with valued recreational time, the opportunity cost can be substantial.

In addition to out-of-pocket costs and opportunity costs, there are psychic costs—the amount of anxiety that a learner perceives he or she may incur by participating. Wasson (1975) notes five conditions that are general sources of anxiety: uncertainty, rejection, frustration and conflict, cognitive dissonance, and physical harm. Consider the uncertainty that an older adult may feel when participating in a course with mostly younger students, the rejection a high school dropout may re-experience when returning to the same school for literacy classes, the frustration one feels upon being late because there was no parking, the cognitive dissonance a re-entry woman may experience in attending her first employer's training sequence. Obviously, these costs may be substantial indeed.

If marketing is the art and science of managing exchange relationships, several things must occur prior to success. First, we must understand the learner—his or her needs, interests, and costs likely to be incurred through participation. Likewise, we must understand the things that compete for learners' participation. These are the objectives of *market research*. Second, *products* that meet learner needs, interests, and preferences must be developed. This is the purpose of product development. Third, communication must be established with the learner—the role of *promotion*. Finally, we must present our offerings at an acceptable cost to the learner. This means the establishment of a viable *price* and locating our programs in an accessible *place*, reducing opportunity costs. Market research provides the information, and the four P's of product, promotion, place, and price provide the tools. From a practical standpoint, the objective of marketing is to create the blend of these "tool" factors that will create the most advantageous exchange relationships. Clearly, all four factors are interrelated. For example, if one develops a product with high instructor costs in a "plush" location, the quality level may be high, but also the price. Likewise, to hold price at a minimum, a subsidy may be required or other product costs must be minimized.

Market Segmentation

Equipped with these basic concepts—exchange and the four P's—we now confront a dilemma. Although we want to create exchange, we know that different types of people are likely to respond to the four P's in different ways. How can that problem be resolved? The answer is through market segmentation, a critical step in marketing.

Market segmentation is a process of dividing the potential market into subgroups according to how they are expected to react to program offerings. Each should be potentially reachable by a specific mix of the four P's. Although there is no established formula for segmentation, three sets of segmentation variables are commonly used: geographic, demographic, and psychographic. Geographic variables include such things as the distance of potential learners from the program site, as well as urban, suburban, or rural places of residence. Demographic variables pertain to age, sex, income, prior education, occupation, and so forth. Psychographic variables relate to individual behavior patterns, such as life-style, personality, and benefits sought. Once the market has been segmented, the next step is to decide how many of the segments will be served with different blends of product, price, promotion, and place. If the whole market is treated as one homogeneous group, which is tantamount to ignoring segmentation, *undifferentiated marketing* results. If one segment is selected for special attention, *concentrated marketing* occurs. If the continuing education unit offers programs in two or more segments, this is termed *differentiated marketing*.

Undifferentiated marketing is counterproductive, according to the marketing approach. Concentrated marketing—servicing one particularly important, needy, or high-demand group—is sometimes effective, especially if the continuing education unit is relatively new and lacks the resources to serve more than one segment. Generally speaking, however, differentiated marketing will produce the best results and the best service.

For example, Eastern University's Graduate School of Education is research-oriented, primarily serving public school educators with master's and doctoral programs. The continuing education program operated by the school is relatively new and until lately had followed a relatively undifferentiated marketing strategy, partially in response to confusion over the mission of the school and the continuing education unit. Recently the school was reorganized, and the mission of the school was clarified. Eastern was to emphasize research and scholarship, and continuing education was to follow suit.

Market segmentation, in light of the redefined orientation of the continuing education program, proceeded as follows: The potential market consisted of all persons serving in educational roles, ranging from industrial trainers to public school librarians. Consequently, the first segmentation was based on work-role setting—public school educators versus trainers in government, health care, and industry. Given the school's resources, historic orientation, and the expectation of external groups, it was decided to concentrate on the public school market first. Since the school's new orientation was decidedly "academic," the public school market was further segmented on a psychographic basis into those public school educators who had a theoretical-scholarly orientation versus those who did not. Three general segments then resulted: trainers in non–public school settings, public school educators with scholarly orientations, and public school educators with nonscholarly orientations. The scholarly public school educators were the smallest segment, but—given the school's new mission, the newness and relatively low capacity of the continuing education unit, and the fact that there was virtually no competition for the market—a concentrated marketing approach was selected and focused on the scholarly group. Following segmentation, a series of thirty academically oriented presentations by the school's research faculty were planned at between two and three hours in duration and held on campus for the price of $15 each. A promotional campaign was planned to emphasize the excitement of learning new, state-of-the-art knowledge in education.

Market Position and Consumer Analysis

Once the continuing education unit has identified the segments of its potential market that it might well serve, it must then determine the proper mix of product, promotion, price, and place that will yield maximum participation. This entails two processes that depend heavily on formal and informal market research: market positioning and consumer analysis. In market positioning, the continuing education unit analyzes the competition in order to determine the niche in which it might most successfully operate with respect to other providers. Clearly, this is important; even the best programs will find success problematic in highly competitive markets, especially if competitors are experienced and well established.

For example, James County College's continuing education program is empowered to offer virtually any program within the boundaries of James County. By attending local American Society for Training and Development meetings, having informal conversations with directors of other programs, and systematically collecting brochures and analyzing other programs, the director of continuing education determined that there were three other groups of providers in the county: public school programs that specialized in recreational offerings for local residents; private consultants who provided general management training, such as communication skills and time management, to industry; and the cooperative education service, which offered a variety of programs revolving around agriculture and home management. Public school programs were heavily subscribed. Some private consultants were very successful; others were less so, and the Cooperative Extension Service barely met its enrollmment goals. Furthermore, in addition to content, the market seemed to be characterized by two other dimensions: price and prestige. Public school programs were of low price and low prestige. Consultant-offered programs were of high price and moderate prestige, and the Cooperative Extension Service programs were of moderate prestige and low price.

After assessing the situation, the director of James County College's continuing education unit decided to adopt a market position of high prestige and moderate price, with offerings in industrial management and recreational and vocational subjects. Her rationale was as follows:

1. There was no other high-prestige provider in the market. Since the college was the only institution of higher education in the county, its position could be exploited.

2. A moderate pricing structure would allow James County College's programs to be competitive with private consultants. Given greater prestige, the college's programs would also be competitive with public schools.

3. The college lacked the resources to compete directly with the Cooperative Extension Service.

4. No other provider was offering vocational subjects.

Consumer Analysis

Needs, Wants, and Demands. In order for a learner to relinquish valued resources to participate in continuing education, four conditions must be met. The learner must need the program, want the program, believe that the program will meet needs and desires, and prefer the provider of the program over all others. Knowledge of learners' needs, wants, beliefs, and preferences is therefore vital to successful marketing.

The distinction among needs, wants, beliefs, and preferences raises several important conceptual problems. If, for example, a need is defined as the difference between a desired and an actual state, there is an immediate difficulty, for needs exist at several levels: at the level of society as a whole, at the institutional level, and at the individual level. Just because a need exists at the societal level—the need for literacy, for example—there is no guarantee that individuals will perceive that need as their own or want literacy education even if they do perceive the social need. Likewise, individuals frequently have latent needs, needs of which they are unaware. This is a major problem in public health education. Since unhealthy behavior does not result in physical symptoms until sometime in the future, the need is not recognized until it is too late to intervene through education. Hence, a major objective of public health education is to create an awareness of need.

In concentrating on voluntary exchanges with markets of learners, it is clearly important to identify learners' perceived needs and wants, for these are the factors that motivate participation and translate into demand for a program's offerings. Kotler (1975) notes several demand states, the most important being "negative," "no," and "latent" demand. In negative demand, the learner actualy seeks to avoid the program offered. Negative demand is often a problem when there is a solid social or institutional need that is not perceived as such by the individual. For example, although students often complain that much college teaching is mediocre, staff development targeted at improving college instructors' teaching skills is practically nonexistent, for professors consider themselves experts and see such training as belittling. In negative demand, the task is to identify the source of resistance and, if possible, to change it.

In a "no demand" state, learners are indifferent to the education offered. Although they would not avoid it, neither would they seek it. Kotler (1975) notes three strategies for dealing with no demand: (1) connect the offering with some existing need in the marketplace (2) alter the environment so that the program becomes valued in the environment, and (3) promote more substantially, in the hope that lack of demand is just a function of low exposure.

The third important demand state is latent demand. In this case, there exists a genuine perceived need and want for a particular offering, but no offering exists to meet the demand. The response here is obvious—program development. Continuing educators who are able to tap latent demand generally find themselves immediately successful, as they are operating in a situation of high motivation to participate and virtually no competition.

Assessment. Assessment, or measurement, of learners' needs, wants, beliefs, and preferences can be divided into two types: formal and informal. Formal needs assessment is a form of applied research and must conform to the rules of formal research if valid and reliable results are to be obtained. Generally speaking, unless the continuing educator has substantial research experience, it is advisable to confer with a knowledgeable consultant in designing and conducting a formal assessment.

There are two general approaches to formal assessment: quantitative and qualitative. In quantitative assessment, the continuing educator typically hypothesizes that a set of needs exists and then sets out to measure the degree to which the needs do exist. Usually a survey or structured interviews are employed. The advantages of this approach are efficiency and simplicity in data analysis. Large numbers of respondents can be polled relatively easily, and the meaning of results is generally clear. There are two common problems, however. First, unless research of this type is conducted properly, the results may be misleading. Second, the assessor receives only data on what is asked. Thus, if the questions posed are irrelevant to learners' real needs and wants, irrelevant results follow.

Qualitative assessment relies on open-ended questions administered either through probing interviews, open-ended surveys, or such projective techniques as sentence completion. Although the assessor gets more complete (and probably more valid) information from qualitative methods, and gains information useful in identifying needs that are unanticipated and beneath the surface, interpretation of data is time-consuming and often subjective.

Informal assessment depends on the systematic gathering of data from multiple sources readily accessible to the continuing educator. This type of assessment should be conducted systematically, on a continuous basis. When several sources point to a need, a want, a belief, or a perception, the data are accepted as valid. When sources conflict, additional confirming or disconfirming information is sought. Examples of sources of informal needs data include informal interviews with students, instructors, and employers; analysis of enrollment statistics; feedback at meetings of community groups and professional associations; newspaper articles; research literature; observation of potential learners' workplaces or communities; and advisory councils.

Product

At this juncture, let us assume that consumer analysis has been conducted and the market has been divided into viable segments, some that the continuing education unit is already serving and others it would like to reach. With respect to program offerings, there are essentially four strategies to follow (Ansoff, 1957): market penetration, market development, product development, and diversification.

In market penetration, the continuing education unit seeks to increase its share of the market for its present programs. In market development, the continuing education unit seeks to take its offerings into new markets. In product development, it seeks to create new, improved offerings for its present markets. In product diversification, the continuing education unit seeks new markets with new offerings. In following these strategies, there are three decisions that need to be made regarding offerings: program addition, program modification, and program elimination. Program addition is typically the most risky decision, because it is difficult to know in advance what learners' reactions will be. Especially if the capital costs of developing new offerings are high, it is wise to conduct solid consumer analysis in developing new offerings. Test marketing of new offerings before substantial funds are committed to larger-scale promotion is generally a good idea.

Program modification generally entails a change in the tangible elements of a program that may be affecting participation, such as program title, description, time, and location. Obviously, it is wiser to modify those parts of a program prior to learners' participation. Location, for example, is easier to change than teaching style of instructors.

Program elimination should occur when demand for a program has declined, either because the need addressed no longer exists or because of very unfavorable competition. Program elimination is an important option, as low-demand programs sap valuable resources for very little return on investment.

Two dimensions of all program offerings are embodied in the concepts *tangible* and *core product*. The tangible product is represented by parts of the program visible to the learner and includes such things as quality level and such features as meals and social hours, "brand name," and packaging. With respect to the tangible product, the objective in program development is to enhance visible aspects as much as possible at the lowest additional cost. For example, low-cost features—high-quality nametags, photocopied handouts, lists of participants' names and addresses, and a warm greeting upon arrival—can add significantly to learner satisfaction at little additional cost. Likewise, a continuing education unit with a low-prestige or unknown "brand name" might elect to cosponser programs with another institution whose "brand name" is more prestigious and established.

The second dimension of product is the core product, the essential benefit a learner is seeking in participation. This concept is critical, as the core product motivates participation. When business executives participate in continuing education, for example, their underlying motivation—their core product—is career advancement. When learners participate in exercise classes, the core products are enhanced attractiveness and better health; the tangible product—in this case, exercise—is often something to be endured.

The tangible product is by no means unimportant. Generally speaking, though, program development should revolve around the core product. Programs for business executives should project the aura of "success" in their ambience and in their promotional materials. Programs designed to promote better health and attrativeness, such as exercise classes, might include feedback to learners regarding how much better they now look, as well as biological feedback, such as before-and-after measurement of blood pressure.

One final note: Of all the tools in the marketing mix of product, promotion, price, and place, product is the most important for continuing educators. This is true because a quality program at a fair price builds program credibility and establishes prestige, two of the most vital attributes a continuing education unit can possess.

Promotion

Once a series of programs has been developed that addresses the needs, wants, beliefs, and perceptions of identified market segments, the existence, quality, and nature of these programs must be communicated to potential learners. This is the function of promotion. There are five basic means of promotion: advertising, publicity, direct face-to-face communication, atmospherics, and incentives. Advertising is paid communication; it includes brochures and media advertising. The advantages of advertising are that the continuing education unit has direct control over the message and that advertising has a broad reach—it can reach large numbers of potential learners. The disadvantages are cost and a low degree of perceived veracity from the consumers' perspective. Publicity amounts to positive messages about the program that are orchestrated by the continuing education unit through the mass media—newspapers, radio, and television. Publicity is paid for by these media, and it has higher veracity since it appears as news, yet the continuing education unit has less control over the message and the media have no obligation to carry it. Hence, this method is sometimes unreliable. Face-to-face communication has various forms, such as direct selling and orchestrated word-of-mouth communication, which, if planned correctly, can be very effective. Face-to-face communication can convey very complete messages, and since it is the only promotion method that features two-way communication, the promoter can tailor the message in reaction to potential consumers' responses. However, it is time-consuming and often expensive. Atmospherics are embodied in the messages the program's location conveys. For example, a very plush location may convey the image of quality, comfort, and prestige. Although atmospherics should by no means be ignored, they can be an expensive mode of promotion. Furthermore, the goal of publicity is to persuade the learner to participate, and atmospherics generally cannot be experienced until after the decision to participate has been made.

Incentives are things of economic value added to a program to increase its appeal. They may be tangible, such as T-shirts, pens, calendars, and the like, or they may take the generally more effective form of price incentive—for example, discounts for early registration and multiple enrollments or gift certificates for returning enrollees. Although use of incentives makes pricing more complex, they can be very effective and deserve consideration as a promotional strategy.

In planning promotion, the interrelated issues of what message will be delivered through what channel, to whom, and for what effect are paramount. As Rogers (1962) notes, there are several stages consumers go through in adopting such products as continuing education programs: awareness, trial, evaluation, and adoption. On the basis of the state of learner demand for the program, the message may be targeted at any of these stages. For example, if there is a strong latent demand for a program, creating awareness should be sufficient. If, however, there is little demand for a good program, the message may have to be geared to awareness and to inducing trial. Returning enrollees have completed the evaluation stage, and messages to them should emphasize positive past experiences. Finally, those who have actually "adopted" the skills and knowledge of previous programs may be of great assistance in word-of-mouth promotion efforts.

The "to whom" decision is perhaps the most critical. First and foremost, publicity should be geared to the salient attributes of the target market segment. For example, although elegant language in advertising may attract the highly educated, it may repel the less educated. Likewise, businessmen respond well to glossy brochures, while those in the public service sector respond better to a nonglossy paper. In considering the "to whom," it is important to bear in mind the core product—the essential benefit the learner is seeking. The message and the medium should be selected accordingly. For programs whose core product is escape from the pressures of daily life, for example, the message might convey a spirit of romance and fun, and the channel might be one that reaches people when they are ready to relax.

Obviously, the channel, or medium, of the message should be one that reaches the greatest concentration of the target segments at the time they are most disposed toward making the decision to participate. Information about which media are most attended to should be part of consumer analysis. In program evaluation, it is generally useful to ask participants how they learned of the program. Timing of the message is vital. Generally speaking, the more complex the arrangements learners need to make, the earlier they must receive the message. Also, the more messages potential learners receive through different channels, the more likely is their decision to participate.

Place

Two key dimensions of deciding whether to participate in continuing education are the questions of what will be learned and where. The *where* pertains to location. There are two aspects of location: the tangible costs and benefits associated with it, and its symbolic value. Both are important.

In making the decision to participate, potential learners weigh the tangible benefits of location—its comfort, its interest, and its convenience—against the out-of-pocket and opportunity cost involved in getting there. A location should be selected only after careful analysis of costs and benefits to the learner. Generally speaking, the key issues regarding tangible costs and benefits are accessibility and attention to the special attributes of the target market segment. Obvious, but frequently ignored, is the necessity of good lighting and sound acoustics for elderly learners, as well as easy access to the instructional site.

The symbolic value of a location is frequently as important as or more important than the tangible aspects. Strong attitudes and beliefs are frequently associated with a program site. For example, high school dropouts who have "failed" at public schooling may be reluctant to return to the public school—the place of failure—for adult education classes, and physicians whose self-images include elements of prestige react better to locations that convey prestige. Although conducting continuing education at the place of work has many tangible benefits, such as convenience, if the work setting has adverse symbolic value, it is better to select another location.

Price

Pricing is a vital function of marketing, not only because price is a critical element of exchange but also because price in relation to participation level determines the income of the continuing education unit. The first step in pricing is to determine the pricing objective. Is the continuing education unit willing to lose money on a program that yields benefits more important than income? Does it wish to break even, or does it wish to maximize income? Once this decision is made, there are basically three methods for fixing a price: cost-oriented, demand-oriented, and competition-oriented pricing. Typically, continuing education units consider all three.

In cost-oriented pricing, the cost of a program is determined, a projection of anticipated attendance is made, and, in accordance with pricing objectives, a fee is set by reconciling projected income with projected costs. Accurate cost and enrollment projections are obviously critical.

In projecting costs, it is important to distinguish between and account for sunk and variable costs. Sunk costs are costs the program must incur whether or not it runs. They include, for example, the indirect costs of telephones and salaried employees, as well as all expenditures, such as promotional expenses, that occur prior to the program. Variable costs are those incurred only if the program is conducted, such as food service and room rental. Frequently, programs that adopt a cost-oriented pricing strategy adopt policies of cancelling a program if it appears that enrollment fees will be insufficient to meet pricing objectives. If sunk costs are high, however, this presents a real dilemma, because sunk costs must be paid regardless of whether the program is conducted. Thus, it is often better to conduct the program, even if there will be a small loss, than to cancel the program and incur the entire sunk costs.

Clearly, accurate cost projection is only one ingredient of cost-oriented pricing; the other is accurate enrollment projection. The best data for enrollment projection are derived from prior experience with similar programs for the same target market. In offering new programs to new markets, pricing is risky. It is advisable to keep sunk costs at a minimum until the market potential is known.

In demand-oriented pricing, the continuing education unit charges what the market will bear. It is quite common, for example, for a continuing education unit to have a two-tiered pricing structure, with a higher price charged to industry than to the public sector. Industry is willing or at least able to pay more.

It is quite difficult to ascertain what the market will bear in terms of price, and most units that use this kind of pricing typically arrive at a price through incremental experimentation. Relevant here is the issue of elasticity, which is a measure of the ratio between rising price and participation. When price can be raised and participation declines so little that increased revenue results, then the market can bear a greater price. However, if participation falls when price is increased, to the extent that net income declines, then the maximum demand-oriented price has been exceeded.

The final pricing method is competition-oriented pricing. In this case, the continuing education unit charges what the competition charges. Although it is generally not difficult to determine what providers of similar offerings charge—most advertise their prices in promotional literature—it is important to consider generic competition as well. Generic competition is competition from other products that fulfill the same desires as continuing education. For example, avocational continuing education probably competes more with other forms of recreation, such as the movies, than it does with other forms of continuing education. This should be taken into account in competition-oriented pricing.

Conclusion

Marketing is an organizational strategy that entails planned and orchestrated efforts to create the circumstances under which learners are willing to exchange their valued resources for continuing education offerings they value more. To create exchange, continuing educators must first understand the needs, wants, and preferences of target markets. They must then develop strategic plans for blending products, promotion, location, and price into coherent offerings that appeal to identified market segments. Marketing must proceed in an atmosphere of continuous assessment and planning, in accordance with the mission of the larger institution. Marketing planned and implemented in this way is a powerful tool for programs' success.

References

Ansoff, I. H. "Strategies for Diversification." *Harvard Business Review*, September/October 1957, 113-127.

Kotler, P. *Marketing for Non-Profit Organizations.* Englewood Cliffs, N.J.: Prentice-Hall, 1975.

Rados, D. L. *Marketing for Nonprofit Organizations.* Boston: Auburn House, 1981.

Rogers, E. *The Diffusion of Innovations.* New York: The Free Press, 1962.

Wasson, C. *Consumer Behavior: A Managerial Viewpoint.* Austin, Tex.: Austin Press, 1975.

Hal Beder is associate professor of adult and continuing education at Rutgers University.

In defining markets, the philosopphy, mission, goals, and resource strengths of the institution are matched with the needs of market groups selected for service.

Defining and Analyzing the Market

Wendell L. Smith

Initiating a successful marketing plan for continuing education requires firm commitment and broad participation from throughout the institution; marketing is a team effort, and as such must have the endorsement and commitment of employees throughout the organization in all aspects, including establishing the marketing concept, setting specific objectives, defining specific marketing activities, program implementation, and assessment.

Determining Your Best Niche

Following commitment to a systematic marketing program, the next step is determining the institution's strengths and weaknesses.

Continuing educators are often taken in by fads. This tendency, however, must be avoided, as such mindless action tends to fragment the program, destroy its image, and leave staff as well as students without a sense of direction and stability. In developing a successful marketing plan, one must utilize a more systematic approach in developing a solid, academic marketing focus, which builds image and sense of direction. A major weakness of contemporary continuing education is that all too often we attempt to be all things to all people.

H. Beder (Ed.). *Marketing Continuing Education.*
New Directions for Continuing Education, no. 31. San Francisco: Jossey-Bass, Fall 1986.

Institutional Philosophy, Mission, and Goals. The philosophy, mission, and goals of the institution are important in setting the broad parameters of the continuing education program. Land-grant universities and community colleges often have a more extensive public service and community outreach obligation than do, for example, private research universities. In outreach-oriented institutions, the continuing education function typically receives greater emphasis in such things as faculty rank and tenure determination than in research-oriented institutions. Also, institutions with a public service legacy usually receive more financial support for their continuing education activities because of the recognition that many of a community's educational needs pertain to individuals and agencies that are unable to pay the full costs of programs.

Often, continuing education programs identify educational needs and build constituencies that ultimately result in the formation of new academic degrees at the institution. For example, continuing education administrators are sometimes asked by their institution's chief academic administrators to test pilot programs or develop constituencies that will lead to the development of new academic programs. In such cases, the initial costs are underwritten by the institution as developmental efforts.

Knowing Your Resources. In addition to being compatible with an institution's philosophy, mission, and developmental goals, the operation of continuing education programs must be compatible with the institution's resources. One must, for example, have a comprehensive and accurate understanding of faculty teaching and research expertise. After internal resources have been thoroughly explored, the next step is to analyze community resources that augment one's academic base. It is as important to know which resources you do not have as it is to know what resources you do have, for trying to deliver programs in areas where you do not have expertise can not only destroy the reputation and credibility of the continuing education program but can also create a deleterious image for the whole institution.

Walshok (1982) describes the faculty liaison role as "networking." She points to three reasons why this process is critical: "(1) The best first place to begin your academic program is with the strengths, reputation, and service areas of your own campus; (2) regardless of what emphasis your program has, the prestige, experience, and depth of individual faculty or on-campus programs can be tied in in ways that enhance the academic weight and overall quality of a program; and (3) politically, it is essential to have campus support for an extension program. Programming in support of campus needs and interests or utilizing campus resources in the context of more adult-oriented activities build both familiarity with and commitment to the activities of extension."

The identification of resource strengths and weaknesses must be a systematic and thorough process. This process often involves much more than brokering faculty expertise in its current form; it also involves matching and blending faculty expertise into a marketable form that will have relevant and direct application to the lifelong learning needs of the community beng served. Many faculty lack experience in instructing continuing education programs, and components from existing credit courses often require considerable revision for them to be relevant in other applications, such as noncredit short courses.

Market Positioning. Market positioning is a process of developing programs that match the philosophy, mission, goals, and resource strengths of your institution to the educational needs of market groups you specifically want to serve.

Universities should identify an overall market position for their continuing education programs. The individual courses and services offered should be part of and contribute to the whole, rather than being fragmented and unrelated to the academic base, goals, and image that the institution is attempting to sustain.

Successful market positioning requires a shared sense of mission and philosophy, consistency of organizational goals, uniform quality and instructional standards, and shared image goals.

Assessing Your Competition

After continuing education has accurately determined its best niche and is truly operating from a focused resource position utilizing its faculty strengths, the definition and analysis of the marketplace will be much easier. Nevertheless, a thorough initial analysis and continuing sensitivity need to exist within the marketing environment if a program is going to be successful.

The University and Its Public. There are six different publics critical to a university: competitors, trustees, faculty, students, the mass media, and the local community. The actual or potential impact of these publics on the organization may vary greatly from time to time, but since publics tend to be interrelated, a negative image perceived by one can easily be conveyed to others.

Kotler (1975) views the university as a resource-conversion machine in which the "internal publics" take the resources of "input publics" and convert them into useful products that are carried by "agent publics" to designated "consuming publics." We have discussed the important role of faculty and other key internal publics. Input publics consist of material and service suppliers and the regulatory organizations and commissions that provide standards and criteria for certification. Agent publics consist of brokers, such as continuing education staff, school counselors, and the mass media. Finally, the consuming publics are clients, clients' employers, competitors, and others who either directly participate in one's programs or who are in a position to directly influence student participation.

Competition and Networking. Just as it is important to identify the strengths and weaknesses of your own institution, it is equally important to assess the strengths and weaknesses of others who are competing in the same marketplace. In this regard, a great deal can be learned by reviewing the programs listed in the catalogue and mailings of other institutions that offer similar programs in comparable communities in other parts of the country.

Through networking with professional colleagues, a vast amount of information can be acquired. At the local level, many larger communities have continuing education councils that provide adult student referral services and sponsor such activities as lifelong learning fairs. Active participation in such local associations can allow continuing educators to develop personal acquaintances with counterparts, contacts that then lead to open exchange of marketing information.

A more advanced stage of cooperation among institutions sometimes results in program co-sponsorship, joint use of outreach facilities, and cooperative marketing. This type of cooperation can often be extremely beneficial to public institutions in conveying to legislators that, because of collaboration, unnecessary duplication is minimal.

At the state and regional levels, networking opportunities and information sharing take place through professional associations. Most state and regional associations hold annual conferences. At these events, as well as through newsletters, the "swap shop" opportunities that result can be extremely useful. National information exchange is available through professional associations, workshops, and seminars. Most of the national continuing education associations have information exchange among members as one of their major objectives.

Audience Segmentation

The potential continuing education audience is very diverse. It can be subdivided by a multitude of demographic, geographic, and psychographic factors. The subdivision of a population to better describe, understand, and predict behavior so that more effective promotional activities and programs can be developed is an important marketing process called *audience segmentation.*

Four major ways in which audiences may be segmented include occupationally (by public and private sectors; by trade unions); demographically (by age, sex, education, and income level); geographically (by inner city, rural, or urban residence); and psychographically (by personality, life-style, or interests).

Employment Base or Occupation. An increasing number of continuing education offerings are job-related. Frequently, a business either pays employees' registration fees or contracts with continuing education to provide courses to meet specific employee needs.

Some continuing education offerings, such as courses in first-level supervision or general management principles, are generic to both public and private sector audiences; however, many courses, including the generic ones, can be marketed better if they are designed to be more audience-specific by reflecting content and examples relevant to a specific clientele.

Organizations such as trade unions and professional associations often serve as viable sources of financial support or endorsement for programs. The United Auto Workers, for example, currently makes available $1,500 annually for each union member's educational support. Many professional associations, such as medical and engineering organizations, stress professional development and are willing to help design programs and endorse them to their members.

Demographics. The demographic variables most useful in segmentation are age, sex, education, and income level. A good place to begin a demographic analysis is a review of the most recent general U.S. Census, which includes a wealth of information, such as the ages of household occupants, the educational levels of heads of households, ethnicity, median income per household, and the number of household occupants enrolled in college.

National studies by Johnstone and Rivera (1965), Cross and Valley (1974), and Monroe and Teaff (1985) have found many correlations between demographic variables and participation in educational programs. For example, the higher the median income level per household, the higher the participation rate. The more education the head of a household has, the more likely this individual and members of his or her family are to participate in educational programs.

Census data can be analyzed in a variety of ways against other variables, although accommodations must be made in data analysis. Census tracts, for example, do not usually correspond directly to zip codes. Since zip code districts provide the primary demographic unit for direct-mail campaign efforts, some re-sorting is usually required to make census information correspond to zip code boundaries. In communities experiencing major growth, U.S. Census information, taken every ten years, can soon become outdated. Other sources of supplementary demographic data include utility company records of new household installations and community profile information, which can be obtained from realtors, chambers of commerce, and welcome-wagon agencies.

In addition to analyzing external sources of demographic information, it is vital to maintain internal demographic records. To be most meaningful, the external data need to be compared against the internal student database. You need to know where the potential students are and the extent to which you have served them or penetrated a given population base. For example, with the aid of computer graphics, a map can be developed to show the penetration or extent to which a population is being served (see Figure 1).

Figure 1. Map of Population Served

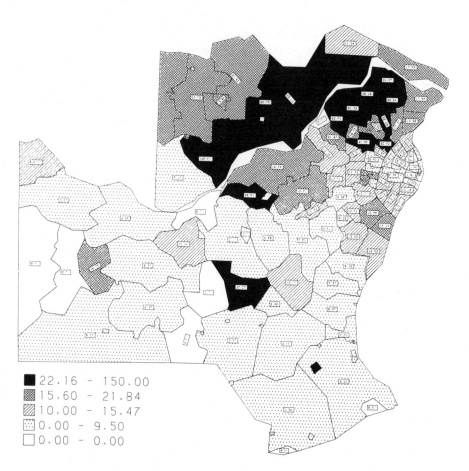

22.16 - 150.00
15.60 - 21.84
10.00 - 15.47
0.00 - 9.50
0.00 - 0.00

Note: Figure 1 is a computer graphic that portrays the penetration of University of Missouri-St. Louis students by zip code in the metropolitan area it serves. The census variable of total students in college, correlated against existing enrollments, can help determine potential locations for satellite campuses or areas in which marketing efforts should be accelerated.

Geographical Segmentation

Geographical segmentation can provide information on where existing students live and work and can provide valuable information on clusters of potential students. Geographical proximity obviously affects enrollments; although busy adults may be willing to attend classes in local neighborhood facilities, they often will not travel to distant campus locations. This is particularly true in communities where there are a number of providers of continuing education. It is unrealistic today to expect a student to drive past four competing sites just to attend your institution.

Also, more and more continuing education students are asking for a full range of student services commensurate with those available at the home campus for traditional students. Institutions that respond appropriately to the course location and service needs of adult students will have a much higher probability of remaining viable during the years of challenge that lie ahead.

Another method of conducting demographic analysis involves a multivariate technique, *cluster analysis*. Cluster analysis groups individuals according to their similarities, the theory being that people who have some things in common generally have other things in common. For example, people who share similar demographic, housing, and socioeconomic characteristics tend to live in similar neighborhoods and share similar lifestyles. Each population segment thus presents similar potential for products and services and similar preferences for continuing education opportunities.

A Classification of Residential Neighborhoods (ACORN) has available a geodemographic market system, which combines geographics with demographics to predict lifestyle. ACORN classifies 256,000 neighborhoods in the United States into forty-four distinct homogeneous neighborhood types, or market segments, on the basis of neighborhood characteristics. With their addresses only, ACORN can classify your students into geodemographic segments. Once this is done, direct-mail and media campaigns can be targeted precisely by zip code district. ACORN has offices in most metropolitan communities. The national office is at 401 Howard Avenue, New Orleans, Louisiana 70130.

Psychographics

Psychographics deal with the personalities, personal characteristics, beliefs, interests, activities, aspirations, and general life-styles of individuals. This assessment moves beyond demographics and general geographical analysis by defining the market in terms of psychological and behavioral characteristics. Psychographics will give a fairly complete picture of a population. It will tell you that certain individuals are doing certain things, as well as why they are doing them.

Some psychographic information can be gathered from general demographic information, available from such sources as the U.S. Census. A "societally conscious" group, for example, would typically have the following demographic profile: younger or middle-aged, middle income, highly educated, and married. A very different group would include upwardly mobile young adults, persons living together but not necessarily married, and upper-middle-class individuals (in terms of household income).

The most valuable psychographic information is generally developed through research on one's own participants. The corporate community has difficulty developing this type of information, but our students are a captive audience, and as part of registration or course evaluations we can find out how students learned of course offerings, whether students are taking a course for personal enrichment or for work-related reasons, what kinds of other course interests students have and why, why students are attending our institution rather than some other, students' personal interests and activities, and students' career goals.

After gathering the above information on a continuous basis for similar courses, a profile can be built of the types of students attracted to certain programs, how these students learn of course opportunities, and what other course interests or opportunities may exist. By overlaying zip code and demographic analysis, one can find out if the students live in certain areas and where other, similar potential students may be.

Image Determinants

The images or perceptions people have of your institution and the programs you offer is one of the essential considerations in market positioning. Kotler (1975) stresses that image is the "sum of the beliefs, ideas, and impressions that a person has of an object." People often respond to the organization's image, rather than to tangible reality. While you may have first-rate continuing education executive development programs, if the community believes your institution is a low-quality, open-door institution primarily interested in basic skills development, then you will find it difficult to attract learners to your executive series. Image is historical in formation and is largely a function of actual deeds and happenings.

In the upcoming information era, more people will acquire image impressions of our institutions through television and newspapers than through firsthand experience. Consequently, through mediated information we have an opportunity to create or to build an image structure, provided we also have programs that can substantiate the image projected. Just as one can convey positive images through media, unfortunately deceptive images can also be disseminated and are often detected. It is extremely difficult to deceive clients as to the actual worth and well-being of your institution.

Customer Satisfaction

Satisfied learners who are likely to return for further study are one of the best marketing sources available, provided you offer sequential follow-up courses or allied program opportunities. Moreover, former students will inform their friends, relatives, and colleagues of their satisfaction or dissatisfaction.

Customer satisfaction can usually be increased by adding values that are not passed on as costs to the student in increased fees. If you had a Nobel laureate teaching each of your courses, for example, you would probably have pleased students. Universities, however, are obligated to provide some level of satisfaction to all publics and must recognize the restraint of resources. Therefore, it is important to measure systematically the levels of satisfaction for each market segment served and to conscientiously see that a positive image is being projected.

Technology Application for Marketing

After one has gathered sufficient data on potential audiences and former students, the obvious next step is to analyze these data as part of market segmentation. Advances in computer technology now make analysis of audience segmentation quick, convenient, and relatively inexpensive.

To accomplish analysis of audience segmentation most effectively, both a microcomputer and a mainframe computer should be used. Microcomputers work best with small data sets; there is not enough room on one microcomputer diskette, for example, for all the data from a U.S. Census summary tape. To avoid continually changing microcomputer diskettes in analyzing such large data sets, use a mainframe computer.

Microcomputer software packages for analysis of small data sets are now commercially available. The utilization of this packaged software can save a considerable amount of time by eliminating the need to program one's own computer. Walsh (1983) provides an excellent analysis of the software available from nine commercial companies.

Conclusion

Market analysis and definition are two critical processes in developing a marketing plan. Market definition begins with an assessment of institutional resources, goals, and priorities. Once the competition has been analyzed and the continuing education unit has adopted a market position, the audience of potential learners is segmented into relevant groupings according to occupational, demographic, geographic, and psychographic characteristics. After this has taken place, the continuing education unit must decide which segments to serve with which blends of product, promotion, price, and location.

References

Cross, K. P., Valley, J. R., and Associates. *Planning Nontraditional Programs: An Analysis of the Issues for Postsecondary Education.* San Francisco: Jossey-Bass, 1974.

Johnstone, J.W.C., and Rivera, R. J. *Volunteers for Learning: A Study of the Education Pursuits of American Adults.* Chicago: Aldine, 1965.

Kotler, P. *Marketing for Non-Profit Organizations.* Englewood Cliffs, N.J.: Prentice-Hall, 1975.

Monroe, C., and Teaff, R. "Using Geographic Analysis to Market Continuing Education." *Continuing Higher Education,* Fall 1985.

Walsh, D. "Giving Demographics More Byte." *American Demographics,* 1983, *5,* 18-22, 47-48.

Walshok, M. "Designing Programs Responsive to Community Needs: Marketing as a Tool for Extension Planners." *Continuum,* 1982, *47,* (1), 18.

Wendell L. Smith is dean of Continuing Education–Extension, University of Missouri, St. Louis, and is a past president of the Adult Education Association of the U.S.A.

*While committed to the overall goal of providing quality
education, continuing higher education must at the same time
achieve the objectives of all small businesses: service, profit,
and growth. Heads of continuing education units must
be planners, evaluators, managers, innovators,
motivators, and entrepreneurs.*

Developing
Program Offerings

Joyce C. Willard, Lee A. Warren

Running a continuing education unit is much like running a business
and can profit from many of the same techniques—strategic planning, for
example. A strategic plan is a plan for achieving agreed-upon objectives
consistent with the mission of the continuing education unit and the institution. It relates the unit's program (or products) to the needs of the marketplace and the offerings of competitors.

In formulating strategy, planners must (1) assess current strategy in
terms of markets and the traditional four P's of market planning—product,
promotion, price, and place; (2) evaluate current and evolving strategies;
(3) analyze the external environment; (4) brainstorm for new ideas;
(5) determine the markets and the products upon which to concentrate;
and (6) decide how to market these products. Using the product-market
grid traditionally used in business, this chapter focuses on the determination of market and product.

Once the market and the product have been established, the plan
must be pilot-tested, evaluated, modified, implemented, and continually
reevaluated thereafter. Programs have predictable life-cycles composed of
five stages: introduction, growth, maturity, saturation, and decline. Each
stage has different characteristics and requires different kinds of attention.

H. Beder (Ed.). *Marketing Continuing Education.*
New Directions for Continuing Education, no. 31. San Francisco: Jossey-Bass, Fall 1986.

Strategic Plan: Product and Market

Planning in a continuing education unit entails the development of a structure and a system of implementation that facilitate learning for adults in a cost-effective way. The result is a series of sequential activities accommodating the needs of the individuals served and of the organization.

Before specific strategic planning and program development can begin, a planning environment must be established. This means three things. The mission of the institution and of the continuing education unit must be clear to everyone. The goals and objectives of the institution and of the continuing education unit must flow from the mission and be agreed upon throughout the institution and the unit. And, finally, the current program must be continually assessed for accurate information and for strengths and weaknesses. The following questions must be asked.

- Who are your market segments? Whom are you trying to serve? What are their needs?
- What are the strengths of the institution, and what are your current product lines?
- What are you doing and why are you doing it, overall and program by program?
- How should you serve the needs of your market segments? How do you market and sell the program?
- How much do your programs cost to establish and maintain? How much do you charge for them?
- When does the consuming public need the product? When do you provide it?
- Where is a good place to distribute the product and for consumers to receive it?

These three parts of the planning environment—mission, objectives, and ongoing assessment—need not be addressed in the order listed here; indeed, objectives and mission are often discovered only after an assessment of current programming. Nevertheless, they must be clear in everyone's mind before strategic planning can effectively be addressed. They must also become part of an ongoing process; they must be part of every agenda, every discussion, part of the thinking process at every level of the institution. Without this environment, productive management of a multiprogram division is unlikely. Planning will be purely reactive and scattershot in nature.

Once mission and objectives are clear and incorporated into everyday thinking, and once continuous assessment has been established, the next step is to devise a new strategy, consistent with the mission of the continuing education unit and of the institution, for achieving these objectives. This new strategy is embodied in a strategic plan that relates the division's programs (or products) to the needs of the marketplac and the offerings of competitors. Strategy is formulated by assessing the general situation pertaining to the unit as a whole and deciding on necessary policy changes.

Basic strategy guides the decisions that shape the very nature of the division: growth of product lines, level of quality, geographical expansion, orientation toward diversification. It determines on which programs the division will focus its resources, where they will be delivered, and how they will be promoted and priced. Within programs, it determines which offerings will be delivered, to whom, and how.

Developing the best strategic plan is a creative process requiring not only the businesslike steps described in these chapters but also (and just as important) imagination and intuition. A successful continuing education manager must have a fertile imagination and be eager to inject new ideas into his or her academic unit. One aim of this chapter is to demonstrate how intuition and planning must be embedded in the environment.

Formulating strategy is a six-step process, and the following sequence is recommended.

1. Assess current strategy in terms of markets and the traditional four P's of market planning: product, promotion, price, and place. Assess whom you are serving now, with what programs, and how you are delivering them. This analysis involves the next two steps and is focused on a new strategy.

2. Evaluate your evolving strategy. Are there markets untouched and programs not delivered? Are some programs declining in profitability and consumer need? Do these programs meet continuing education and institutional objectives? Are they consistent with the unit's mission? Is the staff able to deliver products effectively and efficiently?

3. Analyze the external environment. In addition to the needs of the constituency, what is the nature and market position of your competition? How have you positioned yourself in relation to the competition? What is your market share? How do you compare with your competition in respect to the four P's? Further, what is the business climate for your products? Is demand rising? Is supply rising? What do you project five or ten years from now?

4. Brainstorm for new ideas. With an open mind, consider ideas for new programs, for modified programs, and for possible new markets. How can existing programs be modified? What constituencies might you reach that you do not currently reach? What entirely new programs might you develop? At this point, do not consider the practical consequences; let your mind play.

5. Determine the markets and products on which you want to concentrate. This determination will depend on a thorough analysis of needs

and of market segments to be targeted. It will also depend on decisions about desired product-market mix, market share, return on investment, growth rate, stability, and flexibility.

6. Determine how you want to market the products you have chosen to deliver. This means making decisions about price, promotion, and place. The final determination of market, product, price, promotion, and place is your strategic plan.

Product-Market Grid

Strategic planning in the business world almost invariably includes one form or another of a product-market grid, which in its most basic form is a four-box square showing current products, new products, and markets (Kotler, 1980, p. 79). Although theoreticians have suggested elegant variations on the basic grid, the grid is always useful, for it indicates what the organization has, in what direction it is moving, and what its product-market mix is (see Figure 1).

A variation on this grid is useful in continuing education planning. It permits planners to analyze what they currently have, to consider modifying products in various ways, to develop new programs similar to the old, or to move into new program areas altogether—and to think of each of these in terms of the current market and of new markets. The planner can fill in the grid with potential program ideas and then make final decisions that reflect not only an assessment of the strengths of particular programs but also a mix of new and old. The grid can be used at the evaluation stage, the analysis stage, the brainstorming stage, and the decision-making stage.

Current Product and Current Market

The assessment stage focuses on box one, the upper left-hand box, *current product* and *current market*. It involves a more thorough and pointed assessment than was undertaken in the planning environment and requires that the current product and market be defined in detail. The process involves several steps:

1. List all program areas.

2. For each program area, list the market segment you are reaching, the market you are targeting, and the market needs you are addressing.

3. Evaluate the effectiveness of each program: enrollments, return on investment, growth rate, and percentage of market segment attending.

4. Analyze the external environment for each program to determine the following:

   • Your market share.
   • The business climate. Does this appear to be a fruitful time to grow in this area? Is money available to support such a program?
   • The state of your competitors. Are they firmly entrenched? Are

Figure 1. Product-Market Grid

PRODUCT	MARKET	
	CURRENT	**NEW**
CURRENT	Market Penetration	Market Expansion
MODIFIED	Market Penetration and Product Development	Market Expansion
NEW SIMILAR	Product Development	Diversification
NEW UNRELATED	Product Development	Diversification

they growing? Weakening? Is there a lot of competition? Is the supply of this kind of program high or rising?

- Market needs, both the needs of society and the needs of individuals. Is demand for this product rising, remaining the same, or falling?

At this point, the planner can begin to see more clearly which programs are strong and which are weak. All the steps just mentioned will help to form that picture.

5. Brainstorm for new growth strategies within the category of current products and current markets. The growth strategy for this box is market penetration, that is, the attempt to capture more fully the market for a particular program, without changing the program and without attempting to serve new market segments. Market penetration can be achieved in three ways:

- Current clients can be encouraged to attend programs more frequently. Instead of taking three years to complete a certificate, a student can be encouraged to complete it in a shorter period of time, thus becoming eligible for other offerings of the department.
- Current students can be encouraged to use the existing program to meet other educational needs. For example, if a certificate program requires a minimum number of courses for completion, students can be encouraged to attend additional individual courses after they have completed the requirements.
- Potential students within the same market can be recruited for the program, thus helping you increase your market share. Growth strategy may involve reaching new people, most likely by developing new vehicles of communication.

The planner can now begin to see which programs and markets to maintain or reduce and where to extend either product lines or markets. The final decision, however, should be made only after the entire grid has been explored.

Extensive brainstorming can now begin, with each of the grid's boxes used as a catalyst for ideas. The boxes can be explored in any order, although this discussion will follow the order the grid suggests; this is also the order of increasing risk. Obviously, there is little risk in listing what you have now or in continuing current programming in the current market. Box eight, however, with its entirely new product and new market, involves substantial risk.

Current Product, New Market

An extension of the first box is to expand the markets for a current program, thus better utilizing current resources. With a relatively small commitment of resources, a current program can often be targeted to a new market. If you have a successful current product, it costs less and is less risky to extend the market than to develop new products.

Extending word-processing courses from the general on-campus market to the commercial corporate training market is an example of this strategy. The geographical market has thus been extended. Although secretaries may be targeted in both cases, the range of secretaries reached has been expanded. Extending the market segment for the product is also possible. The word-processing course that has been marketed to working secretaries can be marketed to housewives looking to re-enter the job market. Similarly, liberal arts courses can be marketed to business, to a technical clientele, or to a particular social class. Planners will also want to consider whether changing place, promotion, or price could extend the market for any particular program. Brainstorming should identify as many new markets as possible for each program area.

Modified Product, Current Market

The strategy for growth in box three involves both market penetration and product development; that is, by modifying the program slightly, the continuing education manager may attract more members of a market segment or may persuade current members to enroll in more offerings.

In fact, adult learners seem to expect "new and improved" programs to emerge. Remaining in the first box may produce a decline in enrollments because of a disappointed clientele. Program modification need not be major. Changing the requirements of an existing program without significantly changing the range of courses, for example, can give the program a new look and make it more attractive to your current market. Clustering or sequencing courses differently to form new certificate programs can have the same effect, as can revising, refreshing, and renaming current courses, updating and upgrading the curriculum, or presenting material in individual workshop sessions rather than in a semester-long course.

Modifying an offering can affect the extant program in one of three ways. Modified offerings can replace the old program, older offerings can be gradually phased out, or older offerings can be left in the product mix. If the existing program is to be retained and a modified program introduced, the impact of registrations on the modified program, as on the existing program, must be carefully assessed, because it is important to avoid "cannibalization" of one program by another; the goal is to increase total market share, rather than simply to divert enrollments. It is unwise to replace an old program with a new one unless the latter has greater appeal; assessing market impact is necessary.

Modified Product, New Market

A program may also be modified to reach an entirely new market. For example, a continuing education unit now offering a computer literacy program to social service workers might alter the program to appeal to teachers. A human development course marketed to the general public might be modified to meet the needs of human resources professionals, teachers, or nurses. A tax course for corporations might be modified to meet the needs of nonprofit institutions.

Brainstorming can begin either with an eye toward potential new markets or with ideas for program modifications. This box in the grid invites imagination and tinkering with existing programs and markets.

New Similar Product, Current Market

Currently satisfied customers make good markets for a new program, since they are often looking for additional offerings. A good growth strategy for a continuing education unit is to add programs that are new but still closely related to existing programs. New programs within this category remain well within the mission of the unit.

For example, a unit with a successful program in residential property management might develop a program in commercial property management for the same market, or a program in software applications might be added to a word-processing program for people who are advancing in computer expertise.

New Similar Product, New Market

Serving a new market with a new similar product is a particularly appropriate strategy of diversification. If, for example, it appears that a new program in computer hardware design will divert students from an existing program in computer software, the unit might gear the new program to a new audience, perhaps even in a new place. In such a case, it is of course possible that the new program will simply expand the current market—that the same people will take more courses. In general, however, the computer field has grown in respect to both products and markets, from offerings primarily in programming to courses on microcomputers, financial accounting, office automation, and word-processing.

The health field has followed this strategy. Once it provided only programs in nursing. Now it provides a far wider range of programs to a far wider market—for paramedics and medical technicians, for example. When a continuing education unit concentrating on business management programs designs a new program in pharmacy management or boatyard management or continuing education management, this principle is also exemplified. Similarly, an education department with a graduate program for teachers that has a diminishing market might develop its product by changing its curriculum to serve trainers in business and industry. Often, industrial trainers are technically skilled but lack educational skills.

New Unrelated Product, Current Market

With new unrelated products, strategy moves into the area of highest risk. This strategy is sometimes employed when a continuing education unit decides to extend its mission beyond its present scope.

For example, a college specializing in technical programs may decide to expand to leisure-time offerings for its technical clientele. A business college might decide to offer a Japanese language program for managers, with a focus on business language. Or, as is more likely these days, a liberal arts college may try to expand into business or computer-related programs, hoping that its students will want to increase the number of programs in which they are currently enrolled.

New Unrelated Product, New Market

The final product strategy incurs the greatest risk of all. It also involves the greatest investment of time, money, and energy. Care should be exercised to account for volatile shifts in market demand. The planner should pay close attention to futures forecasting and develop programs and markets that will pay off. The program must be realistic over the long term. Planning against short-term goals alone generally leads to failure and a net loss.

A women's traditonal liberal arts college, for example, might decide that its overarching mission of helping women to be self-sufficient is consistent with the development of a new program in management skills for its current audience and for a new audience of lower-income women. The college might also expect that some of the new audience will enroll in its current traditional liberal arts programs. Thus, the new program can increase enrollment both in its own right and by expanding markets for existing programs.

Too often, continuing education units with falling markets rush into new fields in the hope of staying alive. Many colleges, for example, have rushed into computer-related and management programs in the last decade; only those that moved with deliberation will last. New fields can be exciting and a stimulus to devitalized and continuing education programs, but they must be planned for legitimately and linked to the future of the institution.

One way to hedge against failure in this risky area is to pilot-test the program. Curriculum and market can be tested, modified, and then either deleted or implemented, depending on the results of the pilot. Pilot-testing programs in all the lower boxes is almost mandatory for success.

Determination of Product and Market

Having assessed, evaluated, analyzed, and brainstormed in order to fill the grid with new and promising possibilities, the planner must now determine the programs and markets upon which to focus. At this stage, the strategic plan is finally formed. Again, several factors are involved in the final decision.

Market Analysis. A thorough market analysis of needs must precede the final targeting of market segments. This market analysis is probably complete for all current products if the assessment in box one of the grid has been thorough. A similar analysis must be performed for each of the new program and market ideas listed in the grid. Is this program needed? By whom? Individuals and institutions in the area? Are people likely to enroll if it is offered? What form should offerings take to attract the most learners?

A market analysis can be accomplished by investigating current enrollment reports, surveying professional organizations and prominent leaders in the field, and reading current industrial development and demographic reports for the area. Full-time faculty in the field, advisory boards, part-time professional faculty in the continuing education unit, and experienced staff are helpful in this process.

It is important to consider the needs of two groups. The first consists of individuals living and working in the catchment or service area. By analyzing the demographics of people living and working in the area—their ages, sex, incomes, educational levels, and occupations—the planner will learn much about what kinds of programs will be appropriate and attractive. The second group is made up of people from various professions and corporations. What are the particular educational needs of specific professions? Which ones require continuing training? Of what sort? Which ones require training for job advancement? Where are the additional skills needed? What kinds of job skills will corporations in the area need—now, in five years, in ten years? For what programs will companies pay tuition?

Analysis of Competition. The competition and the business climate for each of the envisioned products and markets must be analyzed. This knowledge of the environment will enable the planner to assess the practicality of implementing the new program. Clearly, no matter how brilliant a program idea is, if the competition is unassailable, there is little to be gained from a new program.

Determination of Market Share. The unit must determine for itself generally, and for each program, what it wishes its market share to be. Does it have to be pre-eminent in the field to make the investment worthwhile? Is it willing to share the market with others and, if so, to what extent?

Decisions About Profit. Desired return on investment for the unit must be determined before strategic plans are finalized. How much financial autonomy does the unit have? What amount of profit is required? How much development money does it have? How much can it afford to lose? Once these factors are known for the division, programming can be balanced between successful offerings and riskier ventures.

Determination of Growth Rate. The desired long-term growth rate must be known. Does the unit wish to grow slowly? Rapidly? Rapidly for a short period? Knowledge of the desired growth rate will balance programming to achieve this goal.

Decisions About Risk. The needed stability level is an important factor. How much risk can the division tolerate? How much freedom does it have to experiment? If experiments fail, what are the consequences? Can staff tolerate instability? Risk? Stability? How steady do profits have to be?

Decisions about Flexibility. What flexibility does the division desire? Does it need to be able to make decisions quickly? Does it need to be able to reverse itself, if necessary? Must it stay on course once that course is determined?

When all these factors are known, the planner can determine the product-market mix—that is, the pattern of programs and markets throughout the grid. Patterns will differ, depending on the needs of the unit. Some managers believe that programs should be concentrated in three or four boxes, to focus energies effectively. Some need most of their programs in the first box; others, more able to risk, will spread the programs over the grid more thinly, including some in the riskiest box. The product-market mix is the central part of the strategic plan. Eventually, that plan will also include price, promotion, and place—how the products will be delivered to the targeted market segments.

Implementation and Evaluation

Once the plan is complete and the manager has decided to implement a new program, there are still questions to ask and implementation and evaluation plans with which to contend.

The first step is a review of the plan, to ensure that it is well conceived. Several questions should be asked:

1. Is the business plan complete? Do you know exactly what you are going to do and how you are going to do it? Are your projections complete and fully substantiated?

2. What is the cost, in time and money, of implementing the program? Is the budget complete, including both revenue projections and cost estimates?

3. What are the potential benefits, in both the short run and the long run, for the organization, for the profession, and for the individual? Review the program life-cycle; look at where this program falls on the product-market grid and how it relates to other programs.

4. How compatible is this plan with the goals, values, and structures of the sponsoring institution, of professions or corporations, and of indi-

viduals? Review the original needs analysis to ensure that this program meets the needs of all participants.

5. How much risk or uncertainty is involved? Review development costs and projected enrollments.

6. How easy is it to communicate what this program is all about? Review your plans for promotion. Are they clear, feasible, and affordable?

The second step is often to test-market the program by setting up a pilot program before implementing a final program design. This is particularly important for programs in the lower half of the product-market grid, programs that are quite new and often involve new or expanded markets. While the goal of the pilot program is to incorporate the eventual program into the standing curriculum, it is easier, less embarrassing, and less costly to remove or modify a faulty pilot program than to delete a fully implemented program.

A pilot program has three stages: pilot-testing, evaluation, and modification. When all the flaws have been removed, full implementation can begin. The program can be eliminated if the pilot shows it will not work (see Figure 2).

At this stage, the curriculum is developed in detail. This process requires the aid of an advisory board specific to the program being tested. The advisory board is composed of experts in the subject area, such as full-time college faculty, working professionals in the field, staff from sponsoring businesses who have particular needs the program is designed to address, or leaders in the field. The advisory board is important in designing curriculum, assessing the market, evaluating the pilot, and promoting the program. It must be chosen and treated with care (see Exhibit 1).

Pilot programs require the recognition that it will take time before the program produces a profit and that special funding may be needed to support the pilot phase. Extra funding is required because extra time is spent on curriculum development, marketing, implementation, evaluation, and modification. Furthermore, students generally are not charged so much for a pilot as for a fully implemented program; at this stage, planners do not want price to interfere with the decision to implement the program. Often, more students apply at this stage than can be served, partly because the price is low. Thus, the unit can select the most qualified students for the pilot program. When the pilot has been completed, modifications made, and the program fully implemented, price will more accurately reflect cost and profit requirements.

Occasionally, outside seed funding is available. Bentley College, for example, is currently test-piloting a program sponsored jointly with a local corporation. The corporation and ten interested companies are supporting this pilot-test, which has enrolled twenty-three students. The companies are willing to provide internships for the students, scholarships, lecturers, and assistance in designing the curriculum because Bentley conducts a program that precisely meets their needs.

Figure 2. Stages of Program Implementation

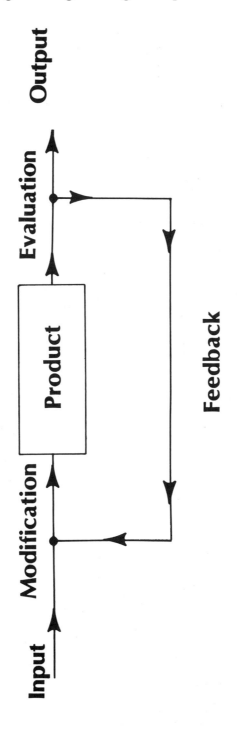

Exhibit 1. Guidelines for Maintaining Effective Advisory Boards

First, check to see that the qualifications of all potential board members are carefully reviewed by appropriate institutional officials, to ensure a good working committee.

Duties and Activities

1. Provide a handbook for each member, explaining the purpose, operation, by-laws, goals, and objectives of the advisory board and the functions board members are expected to perform.
2. Ask the members for recommendations and comments for improving the effectiveness of the board and its meetings.
3. Encourage individual meetings with advisory board members when an administrator or representative of the college or other sponsoring organization requires special information.
4. Invite board members to serve as guest lecturers in order to demonstrate special techniques or skills or to discuss current practices in a particular occupation.
5. Confirm facts with, and seek advice from, board members by telephone.
6. Avoid unnecessary detail work for board members, who are busy people serving on a voluntary basis.

Recognition

1. Send a letter over the signature of the chief executive officer to notify each member officially of his or her appointment to the advisory board.
2. Encourage administrators to reward the board's efforts when particular goals have been achieved.
3. Recognize the efforts of a lay member who contributes outstanding service to the program by any or all of the following methods: a letter of commendation; a press release to local newspapers; or mention of it in major speeches by high-level administrators, such as a college president.
4. Put a nameplate on donated equipment, showing the contributing member's name and firm.
5. Plan an annual breakfast or dinner for all board members and invite a distinguished speaker.
6. Invite the members to college or other sponsoring-organization activities, such as graduation, open houses, special exhibits, lectures, athletic events, and cultural events.

Information

1. Keep board members informed about current and pending state and federal legislation that will affect the institution's programs.
2. Inform the members about special studies affecting the educational programs of the institution.
3. Continually inform the board members about events concerning education at the local, state, and national levels.

Meeting Protocol

1. Schedule advisory board meetings at a convenient time.
2. Send a reminder letter, along with a preliminary agenda of the coming

Exhibit 1. *(continued)*

meeting, to each member about two weeks before a scheduled meeting and invite suggestions for inclusion on the agenda.

3. Make a reminder call to each member during the morning of the scheduled board meeting.

4. Run the board meetings on an organized time schedule.

5. Make follow-up reports promptly to the advisory board regarding action on recommendations made by members.

6. Establish and maintain a climate of informality at board meetings, encouraging full exchange of information.

7. Assign the responsibility of taking minutes to an institutional representative at each board meeting.

8. As soon after the meeting as possible, mail each member a copy of the minutes.

9. Hold meetings in comfortable and quiet surroundings.

10. Maintain a complete file of the minutes of all board meetings. Copies will be distributed to all board members and institutional representatives.

Sponsoring-Organization Reciprocal Activities

1. Representatives should attend industry programs when invited by board members.

2. Encourage faculty to visit and tour facilities of the industries to which their teaching relates.

3. Invite instructors to sit in on board meetings occasionally.

Details

1. Provide parking permits to facilitate attendance at board meetings.

2. Provide members with building maps to assist them in locating parking lots and meeting rooms.

3. Keep membership rosters current. Outdated rosters can be a source of embarrassment.

Recently, these ten companies identified the need to hire people with just the right mix of teaching, accounting, and computer skills. They were unable to find them. With the specific companies in mind, and with their advice, Bentley has designed a program to address their needs. It also has found people who have some of those skills, want to change jobs, and require additional training. Since the program is new and experimental, a pilot phase is necessary, both to correct minor problems before it is fully launched and to test its success.

Continuous evaluation of the program is a crucial part of every pilot phase. It must be examined in detail from the very beginning. This means that there must be plans for evaluation.

Questions to ask include these: Does this program benefit all parties—the continuing education unit, the profession, and the individual? Is the quality high? Is the program administered effectively? Does this program have the potential for an extended life-cycle? Can the program become self-sustaining once preliminary funding is withdrawn?

Sometimes the evaluaton of the pilot program reveals that there is no market for the program, that it cannot produce sufficient revenue, or that the program and its delivery are too flawed for possible modification. In that case, the next step is to terminate the program before further time and money are spent on it.

A pilot program is conducted on the assumption that it will be modified. Almost every program will have problems in design, in expectations, and in delivery. The advisory board that helped design the program can be recalled at this stage to evaluate the relevance of the program and determine any modifications. Sometimes modifications are significant enough to suggest the need for a second pilot-test, again with evaluation and further modification.

The third step is to implement the full program, acting on the plans that have been made throughout the process: plans for promotion, place, timing, price, instructors, target markets, and a well-designed curriculum. If no pilot-test has been run, then the curriculum is now designed in detail.

If the planners have done their initial work well, there is little left to decide at this point, although there is plenty of work that remains for putting plans into effect. On the basis of plans, planners must implement promotional activities, hire instructors and caterers, assign space, print class materials, and register students.

In this the planner will need a time-line, working backward from the onset of the course. It is necessary to know how much lead time each activity takes—how long it takes to design advertisements and place them for publication, when is the best time to publish them, how far in advance a room has to be booked, and when instructors must be hired.

As program planning nears completion, the manager may want to have one or two more advisory board meetings to ensure that the program meets the needs of its constituency and the goals of the planning team.

An important task here is acceptance of the plan by the continuing education unit and, often, if the new program is large enough, by the sponsoring organization. This requires that implementation plans be concrete and complete and that the advisory board be prepared to help in promoting the program. It will help if a high-level official of the sponsoring organization has been included in the advisory planning committee. This official might be a college dean, for example. If professionals in the field have helped design the program, this will also help give it credibility.

The fourth step is evaluation, a continuous and critically important element of program implementation. It will be more frequent during the early stages of a program's life-cycle and less frequent during a program's maturity, but never nonexistent. The results of evaluation encourage program modifications designed to meet the needs of learners and help predict the level of continuing need for the program. Evaluation, in business terms, is quality control; continuing education managers must always be concerned with high quality, as it is the key to success.

The offerings and those who teach them must be evaluated. Managers will continue to ask whether offerings meet discernible needs, are cost-effective, continue to draw students, and meet the institution's standards for quality. Course quality is often evaluated through student course evaluation forms, filled out at the end of the course and, if the course is long, sometimes in the middle as well. Forms vary, but most ask students to assess the effectiveness of the course (whether it met their needs and accomplished what was promised), the effectiveness of the instructor (whether he or she was prepared and able to communicate satisfactorily), and the effectiveness of the text or course materials. Whether the student would recommend the course to others is also a common question.

Instructor evauation is important, both because faculty are to a large extent responsible for the quality of the course and because they are an important part of the "sales force." Often they are employed part-time and not evaluated regularly by the sponsoring organization. Their responsibility for the effectiveness of the course is obvious, and various methods for evaluation exist. Some institutions rely on student evaluations at the end of the course; some require that continuing education program directors visit classes, generally more frequently in the case of new instructors. Some institutions collect and evaluate syllabi; others do not. Most plan to intervene quickly when problems arise.

The importance of instructors as a sales force is less immediately obvious, but they are the student's primary contact with the institution and with the program. A good instructor will elicit student satisfaction and encourage students to take more courses and to inform their friends about the program. The success of the continuing education unit largely depends on the quality of its teachers.

In addition, program and unit evaluations are necessary. A program is evaluated by reviewing the evaluations of all its courses; by including questions about the program as a whole on course evaluations; by querying the advisory board; and by asking again all the questions asked during the strategic planning and pilot stages regarding market share, target markets, enrollments, cost-effectiveness, fit of product to need, and quality.

The unit is evaluated internally by the dean or director, as he or she assesses the work of each member of the staff, and the evaluation should include information about the overall profit of the division, the growth of enrollments and numbers of programs, the enhanced quality of programs, financial stability, and the morale of the unit. Externally, the unit will be evaluated by the sponsoring organization according to the objectives set for it. In general, the unit will be judged on how well it has met the objectives of all small businesses: service, profit, and growth.

Program Life-Cycle

With implementation and evaluation, the development of a program is complete. The life of the program, however, is not. Every product has a predictable life-cycle, although the timing of each phase of the cycle varies and makes precise predictions difficult. Managers of continuing education programs should be aware of the program life-cycle and plan accordingly. Nothing will stay the same; management must think of the future as well as the present.

The life-cycle of fully operational programs has five stages (see Figure 3). Throughout these stages, all programs are regularly evaluated and modified as necessary.

Introduction of the Program. When a new program is introduced, marketing costs are at their highest in the cycle, as the unit seeks to attract an audience to its new program and income and profits remain low. Enrollments will probably not be as high at the beginning as later on in the cycle. Continuing education units must assume an initial loss on new programs. This is one of the reasons for initiating new programs cautiously and for starting but a few at a time.

Growth. As the program grows, costs decline and enrollments and profits increase. Marketing costs go down, as does the time required of program directors and others involved in introducing the new program.

Maturity. As the program achieves maturity, enrollments and income continue rising, marketing costs and the amount of time the program requires are at their lowest, and the peak profit point is reached. The program operates smoothly, the problems have been solved, procedures have been standardized, faculty are well known, the program has attained visibility, and evaluations are positive. Depending on the nature of the program, the length of the maturity stage varies widely. Technical programs in a highly volatile field like computer applications are likely to have short maturities. Programs in less volatile fields—the liberal arts, nursing, or accounting—are more likely to remain profitable for some time; some, such as writing courses, last for years.

Saturation. At this stage, the program draws its largest enrollments and income, reaching the point where the market is fully accommodated. New students, however, cannot be found. The program is fully enrolled. Recognizing the saturation stage is difficult, since program registrations are still high, although the saturation point is characterized by gradually declining enrollments and sharply declining profits. Profits decline because marketing costs rise, as managers try to retain the declining market. Eventually, income falls.

Decline and Critical Decision. As the program declines in enrollments and profits and eventually loses money, the critical decision must be made to eliminate or modify it. Is it possible to reintroduce and recycle the program? Can it be refined to meet new needs?

Figure 3. Program (Product) Life-Cycle

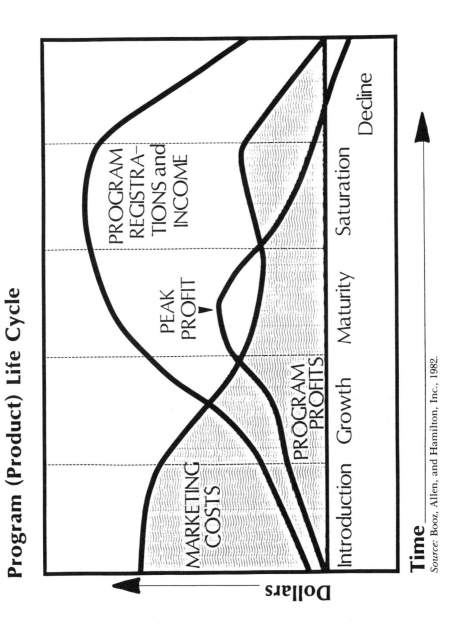

Source: Booz, Allen, and Hamilton, Inc., 1982.

The current stage of a program's life-cycle should always be noted as programs are evaluated in the strategic planning phase. As a program reaches its declining stage, its inclusion in the product-market grid is of special importance, because critical strategic planning for the program is necessary for determining whether to drop the program or modify and retain it. Brainstorming may help in devising modifications of either product or market, or new related products may be developed from portions of the programs that still seem relevant. The program, if it is to be retained in any form, re-enters the entire life-cycle, moving through the planning and implementation phases again to be evaluated for modification, retention, or discontinuation.

The stages of program development are ongoing in nature. A planning environment has been established, and strategic planning never stops. Analysis, brainstorming, program development, and testing are continuous activities. The future and the past are always part of the present.

Business practices and techniques can be profitably employed by managers of continuing education units. While intuition, invention, and inspiration are indispensable, sound business practices can be used to buttress them, making continuing education efficient and effective, as well as creative. It is this combination that marks a continuing education unit as being mature. Continuing education can become a fully integrated unit of the institution, fulfilling an essential social need and contributing with integrity to the institution's larger mission.

References

Booz, Allen, and Hamilton, Inc. *Management of New Products for the 1980s.* New York: Booz, Allen, and Hamilton, 1982.
Kotler, P. *Principles of Marketing.* Englewood Cliffs, N.J.: Prentice-Hall, 1980.

Joyce C. Willard is dean of continuing education at Bentley College, Waltham, Massachusetts. She has had national and international teaching and administrative experience in higher education and is active professionally in the Association for Continuing Higher Education and other professional organizations. Her doctoral degree was earned at Boston University.

Lee A. Warren is a writer and educator who has worked for fifteen years with nontraditional students as a professor of English and as an academic dean. Recent education and writing clients include Oxfam America, Arthur D. Little, Inc., The Children's Hospital of Boston, and Tufts University. She earned her Ph.D. at Stanford University.

*Communicating the value of continuing education activities
in a crowded marketplace to the right prospects at the
right time may be the most challenging marketing
task for the continuing educator.*

Promoting Continuing Education Programs

Charles F. Falk

How to promote continuing education activities is a question frequently
faced by managers of continuing education organizations. Promotion, a
marketing communication process, is one of the four P's (along with product, price, and place) that contribute to the so-called marketing mix for a
product or a service. Making promotion decisions may be the most challenging of the marketing tasks facing the continuing educator.

The challenge stems from numerous and complex methods of promotion, increased competition, increased costs of promotional efforts, and
elusive answers to questions about the nature of effective promotion.

The following discussion is intended to offer practical perspectives
on promoting programs and services. A special effort is made to relate the
discussion to continuing education programs that may not be large
enough to employ in-house marketing specialists on the staff.

Promotion and the Total Marketing Program

What is promotion? Kotler (1975, p. 201) observes that "promotion
is a special form of communication . . . it encompasses all of the tools in
the marketing mix whose major role is persuasive communication." The
function of promotion in continuing education is to present accurate and

H. Beder (Ed.). *Marketing Continuing Education.*
New Directions for Continuing Education, no. 31. San Francisco: Jossey-Bass, Fall 1986. **49**

persuasive messages to prospective students or clients and stimulate interest in particular offerings or services. A specific purpose of promotion is prompting prospective clients to act by enrolling in courses or programs, although some promotion often has the less immediate goal of increasing public awareness as part of building an image. The "AIDA Principle" undergirds all promotion: A = getting attention, I = stimulating interest, D = creating desire, and A = prompting action by a prospect.

Decisions about promotion—persuasively communicating with publics—are secondary to the other decisions organizations must make. A marketing plan must be developed, the organization's image or position in the marketplace must be evaluated, and strategic decisions concerning target markets, services, and products must be reached before attention is devoted to promotion. Kotler (1975, p. 238) notes that such a plan "is an act specifying in detail what will be done by whom, to whom, with what, and when, to achieve the organization's objectives." Once these decisions have been made, promotional methods, pricing arrangements, and distribution schemes become tactics used to achieve the goals set forth in the marketing plan.

The tools of persuasive communication available to promote programs include advertising, personal contact, sales promotion, and publicity. A continuing education manager must decide what combination or mix of these tools will achieve promotional goals supportive of the marketing plan. Developing such a promotional strategy, or mix, entails more than resolving the question of whether to advertise; a "yes" to this question simply brings more questions: "Through what medium do we advertise? When? How often? What do we say? What should we spend?" Again, the lack of simple answers to these questions suggests the complexity and the challenge promotional efforts present to the continuing educator.

Planning for Promotion

Planning processes and techniques offer the potential for continuing educators to use promotion successfully and effectively. A promotional plan can be either a part of the overall marketing plan for the continuing education organization or a separate document carefully integrated with the overall marketing plan.

In actual practice, three types of interrelated plans contribute to a total promotional plan for a college or university continuing education program. In Figure 1, a promotional planning model illustrates these plans and suggests relationships among the three levels of planning.

A unit-level plan is the most comprehensive planning document. It includes all subsidiary plans and addresses actions necessary to promote the total continuing education effort of the college or university. Goals for a

Figure 1. Planning Model for Promoting Continuing Education

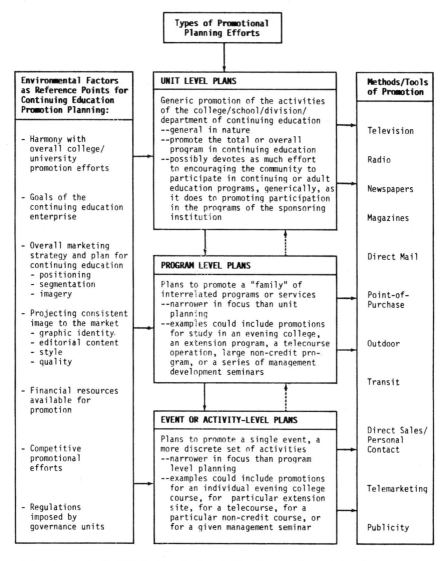

```
                        ┌─────────────────────┐
                        │ Types of Promotional│
                        │  Planning Efforts   │
                        └─────────────────────┘
```

Types of Promotional Planning Efforts

Environmental Factors as Reference Points for Continuing Education Promotion Planning:

- Harmony with overall college/ university promotion efforts

- Goals of the continuing education enterprise

- Overall marketing strategy and plan for continuing education
  - positioning
  - segmentation
  - imagery

- Projecting consistent image to the market
  - graphic identity.
  - editorial content
  - style
  - quality

- Financial resources available for promotion

- Competitive promotional efforts

- Regulations imposed by governance units

UNIT LEVEL PLANS

Generic promotion of the activities of the college/school/division/ department of continuing education
--general in nature
--promote the total or overall program in continuing education
--possibly devotes as much effort to encouraging the community to participate in continuing or adult education programs, generically, as it does to promoting participation in the programs of the sponsoring institution

PROGRAM LEVEL PLANS

Plans to promote a "family" of interrelated programs or services
--narrower in focus than unit planning
--examples could include promotions for study in an evening college, an extension program, a telecourse operation, large non-credit program, or a series of management development seminars

EVENT OR ACTIVITY-LEVEL PLANS

Plans to promote a single event, a more discrete set of activities
--narrower in focus than program level planning
--examples could include promotions for an individual evening college course, for particular extension site, for a telecourse, for a particular non-credit course, or for a given management seminar

Methods/Tools of Promotion

Television

Radio

Newspapers

Magazines

Direct Mail

Point-of-Purchase

Outdoor

Transit

Direct Sales/ Personal Contact

Telemarketing

Publicity

Note: Arrows in the illustration denote relationships and "connectedness" between the levels of planning and also between "environmental" factors, planning efforts, and promotional methods chosen to implement promotional strategies.

unit plan could include creating awareness of the total continuing education program and selling the concept of continuing education per se to the community or region served by the institution. In essence, the unit plan is analogous to institutional advertising by commercial organizations.

A program-level plan is narrower in scope. Individuals responsible for major functions—departments or divisions, programs, and services—within the continuing education enterprise should have a plan describing promotional efforts appropriate to their activities.

Finally, event or activity plans are the narrowest and most specific. They may also be the most prevalent. Event plans promote individual events, or perhaps a series of events, sponsored by a major office within the continuing education organization and delivered over a fairly limited period of time.

Integration of Promotion Planning Efforts. It is essential that all three types of promotional plans be carefully integrated. The model in Figure 1 suggests not only integration but also synergy. A basic concept is that promotion for the unit will provide direction and support for program and event promotions. Program-level promotional efforts should provide direction and support for event-level promotions. Similarly, event- and program-level promotions should be consistent with and otherwise reinforce unit-level promotional objectives.

The many environmental factors noted in the model provide reference points for all promotional activities at all levels. For example, it can be presumed that the chief continuing education official will be concerned about the image of the overall program, and there will be some desire for uniformity in the quality and information included in communications with prospective learners and clients. It may also be assumed that the chief executive officer of a college or university will not want the chief continuing education official conducting a promotional campaign for continuing education that is inconsistent with the image of the total institution.

Elements in the Promotional Plan. Although more items could be included, a promotional plan should include the following elements:

1. *Communications objectives.* Essentially, this is determining what message we wish to send to whom. Objectives should support goals in the marketing plan.

2. *A timetable.* To whom, by when, how frequently, or over what time period do we want to send persuasive messages?

3. *Tools to be utilized.* What communications media or approaches are to be employed?

4. *Cost projections.* A budget outlining expenditures in several categories should answer any questions about projected costs.

5. *Evaluation.* How will we know that we have met our goals? A means of evaluating the success of promotional efforts during and at the end of a campaign period will be helpful to future planning efforts. Eval-

uation can also be helpful when budget approval for future expenditures is sought.

Other aspects of marketing planning set the stage for promotion planning. Programs to be emphasized will have been determined, and market segments or target markets will have been identified. For example, a college or university may decide to implement a weekend program to allow diploma or associate-degree nurses to complete a bachelor of science in nursing degree. The target market—registered nurses who do not have the bachelor's degree—is well defined. The promotional question remains: "How do we send the right persuasive message to the target audience?"

The values of coordination and integration of promotional effort are reflected in the recent experience of staff at the Extension Division at the University of California, San Diego (UCSD). To promote their programs, they published catalogues, used direct mail, and ran newspaper advertising for specific courses. In general, they were dissatisfied with the "look" of their materials and believed that the look was inconsistent with the kinds of programs they were operating. Walshok (1985) noted that "across all of these vehicles there was no consistent logo, art style, or message that pulled it all together and reinforced a total institutional image." With the help of an outside consultant, UCSD formulated a plan with a strong new masthead used on all publications, new typography, and new paper stock to give a high-tech look to all publications. Newspaper ads began to follow a specified format and "were developed to strengthen our overall institutional identity, and not just promote specific programs. . . . The content of our catalogue course descriptions, of brochure and ad copy, and of news media releases consistently emphasizes the themes that give us our unique market position" (Walshok, 1985). This integrated approach to promotion, which recognized environmental factors, resulted in increased operating revenues and reduced marketing costs for the continuing education program at this institution.

How Much to Spend on Promotion

Determining the proper amount of money to spend on promotion is an elusive but central question in promotion planning. Some genralizations provide partial answers.

First, organizations should spend no more or no less than the amount necessary to attract and enroll the desired number of students in the activity being promoted. Second, managers can spend as much on promotion (or on other expenses associated with an offering) as they believe can be recovered from revenue (price, multiplied by expected enrollment). If a profit margin or contribution to overhead is required, then this also enters into the equation.

Finally, building accurate promotional budgets requires that managers become skilled in predicting the yield that will be derived from a given promotional activity. Yield ratios can foretell enrollments, which in turn suggest a level of expense that may be tolerable.

An example would be the knowledge that, on the average, ten thousand copies of a brochure must be mailed to attract twenty-five enrollments in a management seminar. Information about yield ratios experienced by other schools may permit rule-of-thumb judgments, but an accumulation of experiences in one's own institution and market area may provide the only really useful knowledge about yields.

The Tools of Promotion

Continuing educators can use a variety of promotional tools to transmit persuasive messages to prospective clients. Each has advantages and limitations. Figure 2 offers a condensed list of key advantages and limitations for selected promotional methods. This list also provides a reference point for the extended discussion of promotional tools that follows.

The major challenge in making decisions about promotion is to ensure, to the greatest practical extent, that the persons for whom programs are intended will receive information in a timely manner. Choices of promotional media are generally conditioned by cost factors. Newspaper or magazine advertisements are priced according to the number of persons who read them. For advertisements on radio or television, rates are based on the number of viewers or listeners attracted by a given station or program. Critical questions for potential advertisers are "How many persons will see or hear my message?" and "What will my cost be for each of them to see or hear my message?" This concept is referred to as the cost per exposure. The continuing educator's goal should be to achieve a high level of exposure to the target audience at low or acceptable costs.

In general, outlets offering an advertiser greater exposure charge more for their advertising space or time. While the size of the audience is important, it is even more important to consider the kind of audience reached. Once again, advertisers are primarily interested in reaching persons with potential interest in their courses or programs. Paying to send messages to the uninterested is wasted exposure and can be minimized by astute planning.

While other tools could be considered, the following discussion of promotional tools is confined to methods frequently utilized in promoting continuing education activities.

Newspapers. For a number of reasons, many continuing educators rely heavily on the print media to promote their programs or services. For the typical continuing education program, promotion through print media usually means using newspaper advertising. However, regional and specialized magazines or newsletters can be viable alternatives.

Figure 2. Key Advantages and Limitations of Selected Forms of Promotion Applicable to Marketing Continuing Education

Forms	Advantages	Limitations
Television	1. Uses color 2. Uses sight and sound together 3. Uses motion 4. Able to demonstrate service 5. Reaches a mass audience 6. Geographically selective 7. Some market segmentation 8. High prestige	1. High cost for both time slots and production 2. Short life for message 3. Competition with other messages short time period 4. Audience size not guaranteed 5. Selection of "best" outlet in major markets
Radio	1. Reaches a mass audience 2. Geographically selective 3. Low cost in some markets 4. Market segmentation 5. Personal and intimate 6. Uses sound 7. Uses music 8. Immediate and flexible	1. Appeals to only one sense 2. Short life of message 3. Competition with other messages short time period 4. Selection of "best" outlet messages in major markets 5. Listener's attention limited because of other activity
Newspapers	1. Low cost in some markets or for smaller papers in major markets 2. Intense local coverage 3. Timeliness 4. Flexibility—short lead time and frequent publication 5. Geographical flexibility 6. Some market segmentation 7. Permit mail return of information request or registration form 8. Recent proliferation with "insert" advertising	1. Appeals to only one sense 2. Poor color quality 3. Short life for message 4. Lack of secondary readership 5. Read very quickly 6. Poor reproduction of pictures 7. Competition with other ads on page or within paper
Magazines	1. Market segmentation, especially with recent proliferation of specialized magazines 2. Good color 3. Reproduction of pictures 4. Prestige/image enhancement 5. Long life 6. Good secondary readership 7. Permit mail return of information request or registration form	1. High cost 2. Appeal to only one sense 3. Lack of flexibility—long lead time 4. Limited geographical flexibility 5. Position in journal not assured

Figure 2 *(continued)*

Direct mail	1. Extreme selectivity 2. Personal 3. Speed 4. Intense coverage 5. Flexible format 6. Permits mail return of information request or registration form	1. High cost per reader 2. High throwaway factor, "junk mail" image 3. Acquiring and maintaining up-to-date mailing lists 4. Increasing postage rates
Point-of-purchase ads	1. Increase impulse buying 2. Impact 3. Demonstrate service 4. Low cost 5. Use color	1. Limited opportunity to use techniques in promoting a service like education
Outdoor ads	1. Large size 2. Use color 3. Impact 4. Geographical flexibility 5. Low cost per exposure	1. Short viewing time 2. Only brief message possible 3. Little market segmentation 4. Public image may be negative
Direct sales/ personal contact	1. Highly selective from a market segmentation or geographical standpoint 2. Highly personal 3. Very flexible 4. Permit multisensory approach 5. Permit on-site closure of transaction	1. Very high cost per contact 2. Require skilled personnel 3. Extent of geographical coverage of market probably very limited
Tele-marketing	1. Good market segmentation 2. Moderate cost 3. Personal medium 4. Conquers distance problems 5. Can permit closure of transaction via telephone signup	1. Consumer resistance to telephone sales 2. Short life of message 3. Appeal to only one sense 4. Requires skilled personnel
Transit ads	1. Low cost 2. Geographical selectivity 3. Reaches a captive audience	1. Appeal to only one sense 2. Message must be short 3. Market segmentation is poor 4. Public image may be negative
Publicity	1. Low or no cost 2. Flexibility 3. Some market segmentation 4. Some geographical selectivity	1. No guarantee of message ever being transmitted 2. If transmitted, timing of the message is subject to control of the marketer 3. If transmitted, form or manner of presentation are beyond control of the marketer

Source: Adapted from Weinrauch and Piland, 1979.

Advantages of newspaper advertising are significant. Because most communities are served by newspapers, they are a convenient medium for communicating a message to the remotest or most sparsely populated towns or regions. Advertisements in papers serving several communities enable a college or university to obtain breadth of market coverage.

In larger communities served by many newspapers, individual papers may have different demographics or readership profiles. Profiles indicate age, sex, income level, political leanings, geographical area, and interests of subscribers. Continuing educators can use this information to determine which newspaper's readership is closest to the profile of persons for whom programs are intended.

Flexibility is another advantage of newspaper advertising. Advertisements can be large or small. The format can vary greatly, with color, copy only, copy and illustrations, registration forms, or information-request coupons. Despite this opportunity for variety, newspaper advertisements are necessarily limited by the amount of copy that a program can afford.

Alternatives to placing an ad in the body of a newspaper address this limitation. The Evening Weekend Program at the University of Kentucky prints a multipaged, tabloid-style class schedule announcement each term. The local paper inserts the tabloid in the Sunday editions distributed two weeks before each term. This permits the university to economically distribute 137,000 copies of an extended message to newspaper readers in the prime market area. Eighteen thousand additional copies of the tabloid are sent to all faculty and to persons on a student mailing list.

The short lead times for copy submission enable program directors to make last-minute decisions to use advertisements and increase enrollments in programs that have not flourished through other forms of promotion.

Although this may be changing, newpaper advertising has been favored for promotion because of its low cost. Newspaper advertising rates are based on circulation. In many communities, newspaper advertising rates have escalated as population (and circulation) have increased. To make advertising more affordable, some larger papers have introduced neighborhood, regional, or suburban editions. Advertisers purchasing space in these special editions achieve geographical market segmentation and pay only for messages circulated to these special audiences. Wasted exposure is minimized.

Magazine Advertising. Like newspaper advertising, magazine advertisements are priced with reference to circulation. In some cases, magazine advertising rates are also influenced by the demographics of the subscribers. Compared to newspapers, magazine advertisements are expensive. Most magazines are published less frequently—perhaps monthly—and require that ad copy be submitted several months before the magazine is scheduled to appear. These problems may make magazines an unlikely promotional option for many continuing education activities.

However, virtues of magazine advertising include an ability to deliver a message to a fairly well-segmented readership. A recent trend in magazine publishing has been away from such general-circulation publications as *Life, Look,* and *The Saturday Evening Post* and toward a seemingly endless number of special-interest publications. Specialized magazines permit continuing educators to reach narrow market segments in a way second only to direct mail in its precision. Space in regional editions of major publications is another recent advertising possibility in magazine publishing, which may be of interest to continuing educators. Regional editions of *Time, Newsweek,* and other magazines permit geographical selectivity in advertising at rates considerably less expensive than those for national editions of the same publications.

City and regional magazines have also become popular vehicles for promotion. Major cities now boast magazines devoted to local or regional culture, events, and attractions. These outlets seem appropriate for promoting a variety of continuing education offerings, especially those oriented toward the arts and humanities and toward general image-building.

Other Print Media. A fertile field of promotional opportunity for continuing educators can be found in the print vehicles of numerous professional, civic, social, fraternal, and community organizations. These can be magazines, newspapers, or newsletters mailed directly to affinity groups. Accountants, purchasing managers, engineers, city managers, nurses, artists, musicians, and any number of occupational and special-interest groups can be reached through these publications.

Although many groups publish national magazines or newsletters, local chapters may also communicate in print with constituents. Local telephone directories, faculty members, and community persons can identify local chapters of national organizations. Continuing educators may find that their advertising will be welcomed in local-chapter publications and that ad rates are attractive. The University College at Northern Kentucky University is one institution successful at getting space—much of it free—in local and regional publications of the type described. These efforts have helped the university cultivate awareness of their programs in the highly competitive Greater Cinncinnati market.

Radio and Television. Smaller continuing education organizations, operating on modest budgets, may not be able to consider paid radio and television advertising to promote their programs. However, a number of colleges and university continuing education units make extended use of broadcast media as a part of their overall promotional efforts. Using broadcast media requires both technical knowledge of how these outlets function and a substantial promotional budget.

The increasing significance of television as a communications medium may cause continuing educators who have not used broadcast media before to reconsider their media strategy. For example, in 1985 a number of journals reported that for the first time the majority of Americans cited television as their primary source of news and information. This was especially true for younger viewers, who have grown up with television.

Radio and television "spot" announcements have length limitations that promoters should consider. The most affordable form of broadcast advertising is the ten-, twenty-, or thirty-second spot. Such messages are also evanescent; they may not stay with the recipient of the message for long. Also, radio and TV messages are offered in the clamor created by other and perhaps competing messages. Compounding the problem is that prospective listeners and viewers may be engaged in other activities when they see or hear a message. Tuning out during commercials is a common practice and a concern for advertisers.

Limitations notwithstanding, radio and television are dynamic media offering high impact, as compared with more passive media. Television has the advantage of visual messages. Even in a brief spot, psychological appeals can be made through graphics. Radio and television permit communication with mass audiences, and they promote programs for specific geographical areas or selected market segments.

Radio and TV spots can be costly. Attractive time slots are also expensive. In major cities with multiple broadcast outlets, deciding which stations to use for spot announcements is a major challenge. To help continuing educators decide which stations have listeners and viewers with profiles similar to those of prospective clients, demographic information about station audiences can be obtained from advertising agencies, ratings services, research organizations, and from the stations themselves.

The cost for radio and television spots varies widely from market to market, from one period of the year to another, and from one time of the day to another. In radio, the advertising rates will be greater for popular stations than for less popular ones that cannot deliver as large an audience for your message. The cost of a single, thirty-second radio spot during popular "drive time" periods on a major station could be several hundred dollars.

Television advertising rates are influenced by many of the same factors. In television, advertising during a certain program—the Super-Bowl, for example—will cost more than advertising at another time. Even on less popular programs, a thirty-second spot in a good time slot on a popular station in a major market will cost several thousand dollars. At this level of expense, continuing educators must think carefully about using broadcast media.

For those who want to use radio and television, assistance in cutting the costs of producing spot advertisements can be found through the Division of Continuing Education at the University of Utah. This school, which uses radio and television to promote programs in the Salt Lake City area, has produced a professional series of radio messages and television clips generic enough to be used by colleges and universities in other areas. A college interested in buying the rights to these materials need only add its own name, symbol, phone number, and closing message. Other sources of production assistance include advertising agencies, communications consultants, and broadcast outlets themselves. If a college has a radio-television-film program, this unit can be a source of low-cost assistance.

Direct Mail. Direct-mail advertising pieces are a promotional mainstay in continuing education. The principal advantage of direct mail is its precision in communicating with well-defined market segments. To some extent, direct mail also offers the advantage of communicating more information about continuing education activities than is practical in other media. A catalogue, bulletin, or descriptive brochure permits a more lengthy message than is possible in the broadcast media.

Direct-mail advertisements can also encourage recipients to take action by clipping and mailing a registration form or a request for more information. As many experts in the direct-mail field will attest, recipients of direct mail will take action only if a direct-mail promotional piece has succeeded in attracting their attention and stimulating enough interest to cause them to read the material. The material must be meaningful and the copy written in a persuasive enough manner to create desire and prompt action (remember the AIDA Principle).

Continuing educators may profit from brief advice offered by a legendary advertising executive, David Ogilvy, in his widely read *Confessions of an Advertising Man* (1963). He suggests that after positioning your program or offering, "the second most important decision is this: What should you promise the customer? A promise is not a claim, or a theme, or a slogan. It is a benefit for the consumer. It pays to promise a benefit which is unique and competitive." And, more significant, "the product must deliver the benefit you promise." In short, stress the benefits of your unique selling proposition when writing direct-mail copy.

Collins (1982, p. 20) can be a major source of technical assistance with brochure design, graphics, and editorial questions that face continuing education promoters. One practical suggestion is to develop a close working relationship with a printer to "learn how to save money without sacrificing quality. . . . Shop around for a printer who will be responsive to your needs and provide you with consistent and quick turnaround times."

Bulletins, pamphlets, or catalogues promoting one or scores of continuing education programs can be distributed with precision in geographical marketing segments by using zip codes. This system permits mass mailings to every household within an area defined by a zip code.

If a continuing educator has accurate information about the demographics of persons living in given zip code areas, printed promotional materials can be distributed only to zip code areas containing persons for whom particular continuing education activities are intended. This is an excellent way of matching qualified prospects with promotions, and the practice avoids the costs of sending materials to uninterested persons.

Direct mail can be used in a number of ways. In large programs, it may be economically feasible to develop brochures for each of several individual activities. Smaller organizations are limited to distributing a single direct-mail piece encompassing information about all offerings for a term. Brigham Young University's Department of Conferences and Workshops has had considerable success with specialized catalogues—devices aimed at promoting a "family" of related offerings within the total program. Engaging in target marketing, they send a single catalogue of summer workshop offerings to teachers. Time and money is saved, and the "risk" expense involved in developing the promotional piece is spread among the family of offerings, so that successful courses cover the expense of promoting the others. Teachers in Utah have begun to look with anticipation each year to the arrival of this comprehensive and informative catalogue. Other schools use specialized catalogues to promote business, engineering, allied health, and other types of programs.

The Management and Utilization of Mailing Lists. Controlling the utilization of mailing lists—rosters including the names and addresses of persons with special interests or other qualities of significance to vendors of educational offerings—has become a significant managerial responsibility in continuing education. The purchase cost of lists acquired from commercial vendors is high. Creating and maintaining lists of your own is also expensive.

Carefully structured mailing lists offer promotional advantages if they include the names of individuals who, for whatever reason, may be interested in specific continuing education programs. Lists purchased from vendors come in almost infinite varieties. Examples include lists of chief executive officers of corporations, nurses, purchasing managers, electrical engineers, fishermen, preschool teachers, and so on. These lists also can be broken down geographically, usually by states. Some list vendors offer more precise breakdowns. Certainly, if a college in Indiana were planning a program for nurses, it would be advantageous, efficient, and probably cost-effective to buy a list of the names of nurses in that state (and perhaps the surrounding states) in order to send them information about the program.

In managing mailing lists, the key questions relate to cost and accuracy of the lists purchased. Most commercial list providers will guarantee their lists to be accurate within a certain percentage of the names provided, and they will back up the claim financially. Claims of accuracy can be audited by the number of items marked "undeliverable" or "no such address" and returned to the college or university.

Once a list is used, its cost-effectiveness can be considered. Essentially, a list is cost-effective if it has "pulling power." This is determined by analysis that reflects the number of registrants or inquiries stemming from a purchased list. If a list "pulls" enough registrants on a continuing basis, then it is likely to be worth its cost. Unfortunately, it is usually not possible to ascertain cost-benefit information about a list in advance of its use.

Many schools grapple with the question of buying lists versus the alternative of building and maintaining their own lists. Since former registrants are the best prospects for subsequent offerings, it does make sense to try to build a list of former continuing education participants. For those on a list of degree credit students who have not registered in a given term (and who appear to be becoming "former customers"), an encouraging letter is sent, recommending a guidance appointment. A prepaid envelope is included to facilitate the return of a questionnaire in which students are asked about future registration intentions and for suggestions and observations about the programs of which they have been a part. This method encourages return of questionnaires and also provides insights into students' reasons for not registering.

Maintaining a list of persons who indicate interest in your offerings and who want to be placed on your mailing list can also be useful. East Carolina University's Division of Continuing Education attributes the continuing success of its annual "Tryon Palace Symposium" (a three-day program for decorative arts) to its careful cultivation and maintenance of a small but very high-quality mailing list. The list includes past participants in the symposium, friends of past participants, and members of antique, historical, and garden groups. In a given year, 75 percent of the registrants are past participants. The small size of the list and the importance of past participants permit a highly personalized letter to prospective clients, encouraging them to return. Conventional means of promotion are used to augment or replenish the basic list. Special attention is given to maintaining relationships with community groups whose interests are germane to the focus of the symposium.

Trying to capture and maintain other types of lists may not be useful or cost-effective. People move around so frequently that keeping any list up to date is difficult, even when computer systems are used. When computers are used to manage mailing lists, both processing and storage costs can become prohibitive if one maintains too many lists of marginal utility.

Combining purchased lists from whatever source—commercial list houses, community organizations, professional groups—with a limited number of locally maintained lists is an optimal approach for most organizations. Once again, the cost involved warrants careful attention.

In addition to managing mailing lists, there are other limitations to direct-mail advertising as a promotional tool. Principal among these is increasing cost. Postage rates, even for bulk mail, have risen and are likely to continue rising. The costs of the paper, printing, and handling associated with direct-mail pieces have also increased.

Mailing-list problems can be avoided with direct distribution of promotional materials through other agencies, which will deliver your promotional piece at no cost. Occasionally, banks or public utilities are willing to include brief promotional pieces with other items they routinely mail to customers.

There has been such proliferation in direct-mail advertising of all forms that messages about continuing education programs may not make it through the clutter of junk mail found in most homes or businesses. At worst, messages are simply thrown away. The impact of a college or university's message can also be blunted by the direct-mail competition, and the institution's image may suffer from negative perceptions held by some adults about this form of promotion.

This suggests two considerations for continuing educators. First, overreliance on this promotional method may be unwise; other types of promotional efforts should be considered. Second, if one continues to rely on direct-mail promotions, it is imperative to become highly skilled in preparing them.

Personal Contact. Continuing education units, unlike commercial organizations with large direct-sales forces, have not made great use of personal contact in promoting their offerings. One form of personal contact is selling—the face-to-face meeting of an institutional representative and a prospective student or client. Personal contact is not entirely foreign to higher education. Admissions offices have long used field recruiters to make personal contact with traditional students and "sell" them on full-time academic programs.

Fischer (1984) is one continuing educator who has called attention to the contribution this technique can make to an overall program of promotion. He notes that, with continuing educators engaging in a veritable "battle of brochures" to market their programs, it is now time to look at other techniques: "Personal contact should be the cornerstone of any marketing approach. Nothing . . . will be more effective as a marketing strategy for adult learning than personal contact." (p. 3).

Mounting a program of personal contact with prospective clients or students may be one way the continuing education providers can differentiate themselves from competitors. In the College of Continuing Education at Northern Illinois University, experience with a personal call program, aimed at small businesses in the region, was revealing. The business people were unaccustomed to receiving personal contacts from university representatives. They generally appreciated the attention and perceived the calls to be a positive attempt by the university to be of service. A number of training contracts were obtained through this effort.

A personal contact program is advantageous because it significantly abets market segmentation efforts. Sales calls are made on a highly selective basis, within prescribed geographical areas, to persons or organizations thought to be good prospects for the service being promoted. Formal sales calls allow vendors to present a highly personalized, multisensory promotional message to a prospect and to exercise tools of persuasion. A personal call can result in taking an application for admission or a registration form. If the proposition involves selling a training program or course to a business, an agreement can be reached on the spot. More important, personal contact or direct sales permit cultivation of an ongoing personal relationship with clients. Both continuing education and its sponsoring institution can achieve long-range benefits from such relationships.

Cost is the major disadvantage of a personal contact program. Placing one or more sales representatives on the street and supporting them in their efforts can be expensive. Staff members making personal contacts can see only a few clients each day; the geographical territory that may be covered by any one person is necessarily limited. For this reason, a personal contact program should be closely managed. Productivity outcomes should be established and reviewed on a regular basis. Another limitation is that not all continuing education staff members may be suited to personal contact. Sales skills and strong interpersonal skills are required for personal contact. To send ill-equipped persons into the field to perform these tasks is worse than not attempting this form of promotion at all.

The College of Continuing Studies at the University of Nebraska at Omaha uses retired business persons who are skilled in public contact to speak to community groups. They also call by appointment on organizations to explain credit or noncredit programs of the university that may meet the needs of employees. This effort has increased participation rates in the university's continuing education offerings and has led to an expanded use of direct-contact methods.

Telemarketing. This is a form of promotion that has attracted considerable attention in the past few years. At its simplest, it means phoning people to offer information or a persuasive sales message. Respondents can register over the phone for a course or seminar or agree to receive more information about continuing education offerings.

However, telemarketing goes beyond the simple taking of registrations over the phone. It is a proactive and systematic effort to contact current or prospective students and acquaint them with upcoming opportunities that may be of interest. "Cold calls" are those made to persons not currently enrolled but who "should" be interested in what the institution has to offer. While not using cold calls, The University of Alabama at Birmingham's Special Studies unit essentially follows this calling practice. Trained telephone counselors contact all students who have been enrolled in courses during the past year. The counselors conduct a soft-sell approach and act more as advisers than as salespersons. Records are kept of enrollments stemming from this effort. One side benefit of the program is that the Special Studies unit is made aware of any complaints students may have and can deal with them appropriately.

The Center for Continuing Education at Northeastern University uses telemarketing somewhat differently. The goal is to stave off cancellation of undersubscribed offerings. The market is carefully segmented, and a full array of promotion techniques is used. Lists of individuals who have inquired about or participated in specific courses have been compiled, and since the market is carefully defined, a list of individuals to be called in telemarketing efforts is readily available. This combination of careful market segmentation and an aggressive, multi-faceted promotional effort has contributed to a 50 percent increase in one program's enrollment.

The Division of Continuing Education at George Washington University uses a multistaged promotional approach to market its ongoing Legislative Affairs program, which offers both graduate courses and non-credit "briefings." After sending out multiple mailings to the target audience on Capitol Hill, school personnel visit Congressional offices to distribute added information and answer questions. Finally, anyone who has inquired about the program is telephoned shortly before registration. The combination of direct mail, personal contact, and telemarketing has contributed to dramatic increases in inquiries about and registrations for the program.

Telemarketing is less expensive than sending representatives into the field to make in-person contacts, yet it is a highly personal way to communicate with prospects. A message can be altered during a conversation, as needed, and there is an opportunity for feedback from prospects concerning their perceptions of what is being proposed. For continuing educators, a further advantage of telemarketing is that it can be used anytime. Although proper training of personnel is necessary, student employees and support staff can do the task.

Outdoor, Transit, and Point-of-Purchase Methods. For the majority of continuing education programs, outdoor advertising, transit advertising, and point-of-purchase advertising may not be practical alternatives. Since the point of purchase for most continuing education programs is the campus itself (or branch operations thereof), point-of-purchase advertising is not so critical as it may be for commercial goods offered in retail settings where salespeople call attention to or otherwise promote products. Posters or displays at registration sites calling attention to other offerings may have some value, but their contribution to the total success of a program is of limited value. The design and production costs for an attractive poster or display may offset any value derived from its use.

Low-cost transit advertising—placards on buses or trains, in cabs, and on other forms of public transportation—is an option only where mass transportation is available. Geographical selectivity in transit advertising is good, but only short messages can be communicated, and the capability for market segmentation is limited. Further, transit advertising may not be consistent with the continuing education program's image.

Outdoor advertising offers many of the same advantages and limitations of transit advertising. It has the added advantage of making bold and dramatic statements because of the sheer size of standard billboards. However, the cost of billboard space is an added limitation; rates range from a few hundred to several thousand dollars per month. As in other forms of advertising, rate differences are predicated on the number of exposures your promotional message will receive in a given location. Some schools find outdoor advertising effective. The University of Utah uses outdoor advertising to announce registration periods and thereby creates awareness of upcoming school terms. Reinfeld (1977) also reports successful use of billboards and signs to promote summer sessions at Gloucester County College. Part of the cost of ten billboards in that instance was contributed by a billboard company as a public service. Catchy slogans on billboards can personalize the values of continuing education for observers and prompt them to take action—calling for a bulletin or coming in to register. Since readers have only a few seconds while driving to see a message, it must be very brief—six to seven words. Readers may not be able to remember or write down a phone number as they ride by, another factor that constitutes a significant limitation.

Publicity. Next to printing bulletins or catalogues and advertising in newspapers, publicity is the most commonly used form of promotion in continuing education. Even the smallest and most modestly financed programs can engage in publicity efforts to promote their programs. Publicity is the nonpaid presentation of information about institutional activities or personnel by the media. Publicity may be planned or unplanned, and it can be good or bad. Positive publicity about continuing education activities or personnel can be used to sell specific programs or to enhance the overall image of the continuing education program. It can be a valuable adjunct to paid advertising and other promotional efforts.

Planning is a key word in any discussion of publicity. Most continuing education programs can benefit from a deliberate effort to provide information to the media, in the hope that the information will be printed in newspapers or aired on radio or television. The main vehicle used to acquire publicity is the public service announcement, or PSA. PSAs are documents featuring information about programs or offerings that colleges and universities would like publicized. Ideally, a planned publicity effort requires continuing educators to develop PSAs on a routine basis for their newsworthy activities.

Since broadcast media have been deregulated by the federal government, stations are no longer required to run PSAs. This fact, coupled with the knowledge that everyone, including competing colleges and universities, wants publicity, suggests that publicity seekers need to be astute. Here are some suggestions on how continuing educators can work effectively with the media.

1. Know "who's who" at the stations or on the papers. Maintain an up-to-date list of media contacts.

2. Know and understand how the newspapers and broadcast stations work. Know their deadlines and the formats in which they like to receive information, and respond accordingly. Also, provide the media with the name of someone on the continuing education staff who can be contacted for additional information.

3. Recognize that some continuing education activities may qualify for coverage as news items. Understand, though, that media outlets are interested in news, not history. Most outlets are interested in what is happening now at your university. News may include unique, unusual, exciting, entertaining, and important events or activities.

4. Understand that persons in the news business need to be convinced of why your event or information deserves publicity.

5. Recognize that television broadcasters are especially interested in news subjects with visual appeal.

A key idea stemming from these suggestions is that seeking media publicity requires a studied and ongoing effort. Rice University courts publicity by inviting all media representatives to attend any of its continuing education courses free if the media representative plans to write a story about the course.

Publicity goals for the continuing education program should not be confined to communications with external audiences. Internal publicity—telling the rest of the college or university community about activities in continuing education—also deserves attention. Campus political climates in which continuing education programs operate may not be favorable in all cases. When the campus political climate is adverse, it is wise to develop mechanisms and procedures within an overall publicity program to facilitate ongoing communication with campus constituencies about the opportunities within and accomplishments of the continuing education program.

Analyzing the Effectiveness of Promotion

Because promotional efforts can represent substantial operating expenses, periodic analysis of these expenditures is necessary. Promotional efforts can be evaluated in a number of ways.

Adherence to Plan. Part of the promotional planning process involves setting up a budget. One level of evaluation is to examine the extent to which expenses stayed within the amounts budgeted. Since a budget is an estimate, a review of actual versus planned expenses for particular activities or for the entire continuing education program can be instructive for future planning and budgeting efforts. Adherence to other aspects of the plan should also be monitored.

"Pulling Power" of Promotion. Since there are several alternative tools for promotion, evaluation revolves around the relative values of one method versus another. The principal index of the value of a promotional tool is its ability to produce inquiries and registrations for the events being promoted.

Evaluation of the "pulling power" of alternative methods can be reduced to providing answers to a series of questions:

- Does one category of the media "pull" better than another?
- Does one newspaper or broadcast outlet "pull" better than another?
- Do promotions in one geographical area produce more registrations and inquiries than similar efforts in other geographical areas?
- Do promotional efforts occuring at a particular time of day, on a particular day of the week, or within a particular time frame prior to an event have measurable effects on registrations?
- Is the sum of publicity efforts attracting the type of registrants and participants we seek?

Many similar questions can be posed to evaluate and analyze the results of promotional activities and expenses.

Cost-Benefit Analysis. Closely allied to concerns promoters may have about the "pulling power" of promotional approaches is its relationship to costs. To do this, response tracking—tying inquiries or enrollments to specific promotional efforts—must be used. Once done, a promotional cost per inquiry or enrollment can be calculated. Then it can be determined which promotional tools will bring the greatest return on expenses.

For programs operating within large geographical regions, cost-benefit analysis can be applied to questions about the merit of spending promotional dollars in each of several sectors. Will dollars spent in one area create more inquiries or registrations than the same number of dollars spent elsewhere? Answers to such questions can help in allocation decisions for available promotional dollars. In all cases, the goal of analysis is to obtain the greatest practical return on promotional dollars expended and to feed back information for use in future promotion planning.

Image Analysis. The institutional or program image is a first concern of the total marketing effort. The strategic marketing plan for an organization and its efforts to position itself in a marketplace are built on assumptions concerning current or desired image. The assumptions also provide a context for promotional plans. Kotler and Fox (1985, pp. 37-38) observe that "every educational institution has a vital interest in learning about its 'images' in the marketplace and making sure that these images accurately and favorably reflect the institution." They define image as "the sum of beliefs, ideas, and impressions that a person has of an object." Image-analysis studies should be of interest to continuing educators, but they can be complex to execute. Focus-group interviews and survey methods may require skill or time not available to persons operating modest continuing education programs.

Promotional activities play a prominent role in total communications efforts dedicated to developing or maintaining organizational image. Promotional methods, copy, graphics, and overall style must be analyzed to learn if these elements support or conflict with image-building or image-maintaining efforts. Schuehler (1985) relates outcomes of an image study in a small Pennsylvania college: "Since receiving the results of the image study, the Moravian Evening College has begun revising its marketing campaign. Our ads are more bold, more action-oriented, and less traditional. Our publications stress the personal attention available to students and a safe and inviting environment. The results of the study were instrumental in persuading the administration that new marketing strategies would be beneficial."

Using Available Data for Evaluation. Most college and university continuing education operations have or can easily get the data needed for evaluation from within their own offices. Staff training and meticulous recordkeeping are required. Staff members must be alerted to ask (if it is not otherwise obvious) how registrants or persons making inquiries have come to know about the activities in which they have interest. Mailing-list labels should be source-coded. The flow of registrations can also be charted to pinpoint enrollment effects stemming from the timing of promotions. Finally, when registrations are taken, basic demographic information about registrants should be obtained. All of these data would be "in house" and stem from tasks that can be accomplished in even the smallest and most understaffed continuing education office.

Promotion and the Staff of the Continuing Education Organization

As competition in the higher education marketplace increased in the 1970s and 1980s, marketing received increased attention in the academic community. It is no longer uncommon to find marketing specialists on the admissions or administrative staffs of many colleges and universities. For institutions where this is not now the case, Long (1983, p. 104) predicts, "In the immediate future, organizations will accept the notion of a director of marketing, a marketing department, or the same function by another name where the products and services of the educational unit are marketed."

At this time, the larger continuing education programs are most likely to have one or more specialists who concentrate exclusively on marketing and promotion. Since the dollars spent on marketing and promotion are substantial in these organizations, there is logic behind this staffing trend.

Smaller continuing education programs with limited staffs may never see the time when someone can be hired to work solely on marketing and promotion. With marketing practice becoming more central to the work of continuing education, smaller programs will need to acquire marketing skills in one way or another. Employing generalists who also may have some marketing skills could be one answer, current staff members could be provided with opportunities to acquire marketing and promotional skills through a variety of continuing education options.

Help for continuing educators who lack access to specialized marketing assistance is available from several sources. First, a college or university's own admissions staff can offer continuing education personnel insights about many facets of promotion. Second, a college or media relations office can provide the information necessary for an effective working relationship with the media. Third, faculty in the marketing or journalism departments can answer marketing questions or provide direction for the promotional efforts of continuing education, and their students can be utilized in research efforts. Finally, interested alumni working in advertising, public relations, or communications can offer low or no-cost assistance.

The services of advertising agencies can be useful for continuing education organizations without specialized marketing staffs. However, many small organizations don't spend enough money on advertising to be attractive clients for agencies. If program representatives talk with enough of them and begin to pick up the jargon of the field, print and broadcast media representatives can help continuing education staffers educate themselves about options and potential benefits. As a part of their service, media representatives can also provide layout, copy, or broadcast production assistance. Mailing-list vendors can also furnish helpful advice. Finally, the smaller organization with limited resources may find that a few dollars invested in employing a marketing or promotional consultant may reap dividends for years to come.

Conclusion

While promotion is very important to today's continuing education marketer, it must be considered within the context of the total marketing effort. Keller (1983) cautions: "Generally, higher education does too much selling and too little marketing. In marketing, the effort is a more scholarly one of systematically understanding who it is your university is serving, why they come, why they don't come, and how you might serve your students better and position yourself more self-consciously. . . . Marketing is an invaluable tool in helping to improve your institution's communications with outsiders and establish your comparative advantage" (p. 157).

Communicating persuasively with potential clients and students in the highly competitive marketplace facing today's continuing education organization is essential to success. Promotion is persuasive communication, and as such it is an integral component of an overall strategic marketing plan. The need to make effective use of limited financial resources for marketing, together with the multitude of promotional tools available, make promotion management a rigorous challenge for the continuing education administrator. That challenge can be met successfully if marketing specialists can be added to the continuing education staff or if marketing and promotional expertise can be acquired through other means. Ultimately, the best marketing tool for a continuing education program is to offer high-quality programs.

References

Collins, K. S. *Marketing Noncredit Courses to Business and Industry.* Manhattan, Kans.: Learning Resources Network (LERN), 1982.

Fischer, R. B. *Personal Contact in Marketing.* Manhattan, Kans.: Learning Resources Network (LERN), 1984.

Keller, G. *Academic Strategy: The Management Revolution in Higher Education.* Baltimore: Johns Hopkins University Press, 1983.

Kotler, P. *Marketing for Non-Profit Organizations.* Englewood Cliffs, N.J.: Prentice-Hall, 1975.

Kotler, P., and Fox, K. F. A. *Strategic Marketing for Educational Institutions.* Englewood Cliffs, N.J.: Prentice-Hall, 1985.

Long, H. B. *Adult and Continuing Education: Responding to Change.* New York: Teachers College Press, 1983.

Ogilvy, D. *Confessions of an Advertising Man.* New York: Dell, 1963.

Reinfeld, P. "The Selling of the Summer School." In R. M. Gaedke (Ed.), *Marketing in Private and Public Nonprofit Organizations: Perspectives and Illustrations.* Santa Monica, Calif.: Goodyear, 1977.

Schuehler, S. S. "An Outside Perspective." *TACSCE Research Annual,* 1985, *1* (1), 16–27.

Walshok, M. L. "Capturing the Adult Market: UCSD's Experience." *The Admissions Strategist: Recruiting in the 1980's.* New York: The College Board, 1985.

Weinrauch, J. D., and Piland, W. E. *Applied Marketing Principles.* Englewood Cliffs, N.J.: Prentice-Hall, 1979.

Charles F. Falk is director of continuing education and summer sessions at Texas Christian University. He has held marketing positions in industry and has taught a variety of college-level marketing courses.

*Pricing decisions are critical to successful marketing, for price
is a major factor in attracting participants and influencing
perceptions of program quality.*

Pricing and Fee Management

Richard B. Fischer

As indicated throughout this volume, marketing is a combination of activities required to direct the flow of educational programs and services from the educational provider to the final user in a form, place, time, and at a price that is best able to satisfy the consumers' needs. Price is one of the six major variables—product, price, place, promotion, people, and personal contact—that make up the marketing mix (Garin, 1983, p. 2). However, there is no easy answer to the frustrating question "How much should one charge?"

Relatively little has been written about noncredit program pricing and fee management. Few empirical studies have been conducted in the field of continuing education about price elasticity—changes in registration patterns as prices increase or decrease. Clearly, price is a major factor in influencing the public's perception of the quality and relative cost-benefit of participating in continuing education.

When one further considers "that 56.7 percent of continuing education participants pay for their own career and personal improvement education" (Loring, 1980, p. 137), pricing decisions become even more critical to the potential for successful marketing. Regardless of shifts that may take place between individual payment of fees, employer financing, or government support, as the number of continuing education providers

H. Beder (Ed.). *Marketing Continuing Education.*
New Directions for Continuing Education, no. 31. San Francisco: Jossey-Bass, Fall 1986.

continues to increase, there will be more emphasis on pricing as a marketing strategy. Already some providers are positioning themselves as low-cost "discount house" providers, while others are creating an exclusive image with exorbitant fees. Often the program content of both is identical, so that price becomes the only differentiating factor.

Development of a pricing strategy requires knowledge of the continuing education organization's philosophy and mission, budget terminology, key variables in pricing decisions, and pricing options.

Organizational Philosophy and Mission

Effective pricing requires a clear financial philosophy and policy under which the program must operate within the organization.

Type of Program. Is the program required to break even, recover only out-of-pocket costs, recover all costs, or make a return on investment? Or is the program a community service or public relations activity subsidized by organizational funds from sources other than fees? Obviously, the pricing strategy selected will depend on the financial results expected.

Source of Funds. Continuing education activities can be grouped as either fee income–producing or nonfee income–producing. Nonfee income-producing programs have major financial support from sources other than participant fees. This support may come from an internal organizational subsidy, external grants, contract funds, or state and local government per capita funding formulas. Formula funding tends to push prices down to artificially low levels to ensure high participation rates.

Fee–income producing programs include those that create income from participant fees far in excess of actual operating costs, as well as programs that produce income inadequate for self-support. For-profit and private institutions usually derive at least 75 percent of their income from registration fees and are required to be self-supporting (Loring, 1980, p. 153).

Self-Supporting Programs. Increasingly, continuing education programs are required to be self-supporting. Programs are expected to produce fee income that is at least sufficient to cover operating costs. The concept of self-support is probably one of the most misused or misunderstood terms in continuing education. Anderson and Kasl (1982, p. 66–69) provide an excellent approach to thinking about expense and income relationships to determine the degree to which a program is truly self-supporting. They suggest grouping costs at three different levels. Level 1 costs are those associated with out-of-pocket instructional expenses, such as instructor salaries, classroom space rental, teaching supplies, and instructor travel expenses. If the philosophy of the continuing education provider is one of public relations or community service, it would be appropriate to adopt a pricing strategy that recovers only Level 1 costs. Indirect or administrative costs are absorbed by the sponsoring institution and are not included in pricing decisions.

Level 2 costs include all of the Level 1 instructional costs as well as the administrative and indirect costs of the continuing education operation. These might include the prorated salary of the program administrator, secretary, general office costs, telephone, and so forth.

Level 3 costs include all the above costs plus any institutional expenses (overhead) not directly linked to specific continuing education programs. These might include liability insurance, utilities, computer services, professional development expenses, institutional advertising, and prorated personnel costs of central administrators. Only those programs whose pricing strategies generate income sufficient to cover Level 3 costs are truly self-supporting.

Use of Funds. Pricing strategies must also take into account generating sufficient income not only for basic expenses but also for retractable funds and risk capital. Retractable funds are nonpermanent funds committed for varying lengths of time to such purposes as program evaluation, development or refinement, special project staffing, matching funds for grants, and demonstration project funding. Risk capital is seed money for underwriting new income-generating programs or for the development of proposals for outside funding. It is within this context of organizational philosophy, program type, and source of funds that a pricing strategy is developed.

Budget Terminology

A favorable relationship between income and expenses is crucial to the success of any continuing education pricing strategy. This relationship is ensured through an accurate understanding of cost structures and a few relatively simple definitions. All pricing decisions should start with a detailed knowledge of costs. As obvious as this might seem, it is amazing how many continuing education administrators do not know their own costs.

Direct or Indirect. Direct costs are usually out-of-pocket dollars for a specific program or activity. They include instructor salaries, promotion and mailing costs, travel, instructional materials, and classroom rental.

Indirect costs are often referred to as overhead, or administrative costs. These costs are incurred for purposes common to all activities of the organization but usually cannot be identified and charged directly to any specific project with a reasonable degree of accuracy or without an inordinate amount of accounting. Examples include physical plant expenses and such administrative services as accounting, computer support, advisers, institutional advertising, and ongoing professional development for staff.

Fixed or Variable. Fixed costs do not change, regardless of the number of participants. An example is advertising costs. Variable costs, sometimes referred to as individual costs, increase with every additional participant. Examples include costs for food service and materials.

Sunk or Risk. Fixed expenses, such as advertising and postage, that are incurred even if the program is cancelled are called sunk costs.

Prior to making any pricing decisions, calculate as accurately as possible all the costs associated with a particular program. Organize the cost data as logically as possible, so that it can be easily understood. Simerly (1984) provides a good practical overview of budgeting techniques, including examples of budget forms.

Key Variables in Pricing Decisions

Pricing Considerations. Assuming the financial objectives of the organization are clearly articulated, there are seven important pricing considerations.

1. How much does the program cost?

2. Is the continuing education activity a professional-level program for a professional audience? There is a definite price value perception in the United States. "You get what you pay for" is an old adage that still guides consumers' decision making. This is particularly true for professional audiences. Professionals typically expect to pay their own way and look at price as reflective of quality. Most continuing educators err by establishing professional program fees that are too low.

3. Who will be paying the participant's fee? Prices can generally be set higher for programs targeted at for-profit organizations or for programs in which the participant's fee will be paid by a third party, such as an employer. Personal development courses, in which participants pay their own fees, are generally more price-sensitive.

4. How much can the audience afford? There is no reason to subsidize the fee for high-income self-employed professionals.

5. What are the fees for other, similar programs? What does the competition charge?

6. Is the price consistent with other fees for similar programs offered by the same institution?

7. Is the price consistent with other program amenities? If the program involves overnight accommodations, is the price of the hotel room in line with the program price? It is inconsistent to charge $700 per day for a program and have participants stay in a $30-per-night motel.

Estimating Enrollments. A key factor in calculating price is estimating the level of anticipated participation. Unfortunately, there is no foolproof method for doing this. Here are some ideas that may help.

1. Review the prior enrollment history for programs of a similar nature or with similar audiences. Calculate the average attendance and reduce that figure by one-third.

2. Talk with members of the planning committee, opinion leaders from the target audience, or other continuing education program administrators and get their best estimates.

3. Direct-mail brochures may be used as the primary promotional technique. Here are some figures found by many program planners to be generally reliable. If the program is for a regional or national market, estimate from two to four enrollees for each thousand brochures mailed. If the program is for a statewide market, estimate from four to six enrollees for each thousand brochures mailed. If the program is for a general local market, estimate from two to four enrollees for each thousand brochures. This could increase to from two to four enrollees per hundred brochures if the program is aimed at a specific, easy-to-identify local market.

4. With an unproved program to a new audience, it is good practice never to count on more than twenty to thirty enrollments when you are estimating price.

Pricing Options

As Wagner (1981, p. 15) points out, it is not inappropriate to begin with an estimate of the price one feels one can or should charge. Use this estimate as a benchmark for comparison with the results of other pricing calculations.

Leader or Follower. As noted earlier, price depends on the financial goal of the program, its costs, and the organizers' knowledge of the target audience. An organization can choose to be a price leader and charge a premium because of high demand, perceived reputation, and superior facilities or because it is the only source in its market area. It is not uncommon to find price leaders with fees 50 to 100 percent higher than their competitors. Premium-priced programs rely on such factors as status, prestige, and ego to motivate participation. Other organizations become price leaders by positioning themselves with fees 20 to 30 percent lower than the going market rate. These providers count on price as the major motivation for participation. Both of these are high-risk positions because consumers of continuing education are increasingly sophisticated and able to discern differences in program quality.

What the Traffic Will Bear. Prices can be set as high as the market is willing or able to pay. This approach is of particular value when providers have significant participation from the private for-profit sector or when a large percentage of fees is paid by third parties. Only trial and error can determine this level. Holding as many variables constant as possible, increase the price on each subsequent offering until enrollment levels off or declines. This will give an indication of the price range that participants are willing to pay for this type of program.

Cost-Based Programs. Most continuing education providers will focus on pricing that recovers both direct costs and indirect administrative costs. The question in this approach is how to determine indirect costs. There are four basic methods for recovering administrative costs (Wagner, 1981, p. 21): percentage of costs revenues, per-person variable fee, flat administrative fee, or some combination of these.

Percentage of Costs. The easiest approach by far is to review the unit's total budget, separate the direct-cost from the indirect-cost items, and determine the relationship between the two. Usually this can be stated as a percentage. Indirect administrative costs are *x* percent of all direct costs. With this predetermined percentage, the total costs for the program become the direct costs plus the percentage for indirect costs. The price is determined by dividing this total cost by the number of anticipated participants. The result is a per-person price.

The indirect-costs percentage figure should not be inflexible. Under certain circumstances, the percentage should be increased or decreased. For example, for public service programs, the overhead percentage might be reduced significantly. This will have the effect of reducing the price. For programs involving extraordinary personnel time or high risk, the overhead percentage might be increased significantly.

The range of overhead percentage will vary considerably among continuing education organizations. In general, the range is between 20 and 45 percent. Table 1 shows appropriate percentages of overhead costs under different circumstances.

The following approaches to calculating prices can be applied to individual program fees or to fees for such services as conference management (Mueller, 1982, pp. 25–28).

Time Charge. Price can be determined by estimating the amount of time spent by continuing education personnel on each program. By dividing each person's salary plus fringe benefits by the number of working days or hours per year, a dollar cost per hour can be obtained. Multiplied by the estimated time spent on each program, this cost per hour will yield a price for each program. The difficulty with this method is to estimate the amount of time each program requires.

Throughput. Several pricing options try to measure the level of administrative effort in proportion to the size of the program, as indicated by either the number of participants or the number of program days.

Per-participant charge. Divide the annual total expense budget by the anticipated annual enrollment to determine how much each registration must contribute toward the expenses. This can become a flat per-person fee. This approach is most applicable for community education programs with large numbers of programs of similar types and formats and with relatively small direct costs.

Per-course charge. A simple variation on the above is to divide total budget needs by the number of courses planned to obtain an avaerage cost per program. Divide this cost by the estimated enrollment for each course to obtain the individual registration fee.

Table 1. Overhead Percentages

20%	25%	30%	35%	40%	45%
←					→

Decrease if
Project large enough to yield
sizable income
Program has no promotional costs
Instructional costs are
relatively large
Registration process is simple
Little or no risk
Little work required by continuing
education personnel
Public service project
Nonprofit organization
Profit-making organization
is involved

Increase if
Project cannot yield sizable income
Continuing education unit bears
complete responsibility for success
or failure
Direct costs relatively low
compared to sizable effort expended
by continuing education personnel
Profit-making group is served

Participant or program day charge. This approach assumes that price should be weighted to reflect differences in program length; the longer the program, the greater the services and personnel time. To calculate this fee, determine the number of program days anticipated for each program. For example, six seminars, each offered for two days, would count as twelve program days. Divide the total budget needs by the total number of planned program days to obtain a cost per program day. Dividing the cost per program day by anticipated enrollment for each program results in a cost per participant day. The price is determined by multiplying the number of days for a particular program times the cost per participant day.

Risk Sharing. Another pricing strategy that can be very effective in working with discrete populations, such as association memberships, is risk sharing. Risk sharing is usually of value whenever there are abnormally high sunk costs, such as promotional expenses, or when there is a need to keep registration fees low. The sponsoring agencies share the financial risk by agreeing to share equally any losses that occur (including any sunk direct costs, such as advertising) and split surpluses in excess of direct costs. Each sponsor hopes to recover indirect or administrative costs through the income generated by higher enrollments, because the per-person price has been kept to a minimum. The per-person registration fee is based only on direct costs, and thus prices are lowered.

Discounting. Most continuing education programs offer discounts for group registration. Discounts usually range from 10 to 15 percent off the individual registration price for groups of three or more registering at the same time for the same program. While discounting is a successful technique in retail businesses, it does not seem to be overwhelmingly successful in continuing education. Often the discount amount is not large enough to influence participation decisions, or the participant perceives that the discount implies the program was overpriced. However, team discounts are easy to administer and result in some increased registration.

Contract Pricing. Almost all continuing education programs strive to market contract (or in-house) programs. Usually these programs have the cost advantage of little or no sunk advertising expenses. Pricing is almost always quoted as a flat program fee for a maximum number of participants. The client recruits the participants. If the program is a repeat of an existing program, the per-person price will usually work out to be lower than the per-person price of an open enrollment course—if the client fills the class. If the program is a tailor-made course, the price should be as high as the market will bear.

Test of Reasonableness

A key to whether a price is reasonable is to calculate how many people are needed at various price levels to run the program. Then consider whether this number is realistic, given the target audience. One needs to calculate the "break even," "to run," and "least loss" numbers.

Dividing the total costs by the registration fee yields the break-even number. Breaking even means recovering all direct and indirect costs. Subtracting indirect costs from total costs and dividing the remainder by the registration fee yields the to-run number. Subtracting the sunk costs from the direct costs and dividing the remainder by the registration fee yields the least-loss number. This means that any loss associated with running the program is equal to what would be lost by cancelling the program. This calculation is of value only when the program has high sunk costs for advertising. The assumption is that if a program is cancelled, the sunk costs are lost anyway; if any part of the sunk costs can be recovered, losses will be minimized.

Some Final Thoughts

Whatever the pricing strategy, keep it simple. Charge one fee for the entire program; not a program fee and a registration fee and a lab fee and a meal fee. Do not provide budget details on contract programs. Tell the client the program cost and what that cost includes, but do not provide an item-by-item breakdown.

Continuing educators with responsibility for planning programs should have responsibility for managing budgets and the authority to set the fee (Simerly, 1984, p. 3).

The objective of any pricing strategy is to manage resources effectively and provide the best-quality educational experience possible.

References

Anderson, R. E., and Kasl, E. S. *The Costs and Financing of Adult Education and Training.* Lexington, Mass.: Lexington Books, 1982.

Garin, R. H. "The New Concept of Marketing." In W. Draves (Ed.), *The Marketing Manual.* Manhattan, Kans.: Learning Resources Network (LERN), 1983.

Loring, R. K. "Finance." In H. Alford (Ed.), *Power and Conflict in Continuing Education: Survival and Prosperity for All?* Belmont, Calif.: Wadsworth, 1980.

Mueller, G. *Successful Conference Programming Methods.* Jackson, Mich.: Fern Publications, 1982.

Simerly, R. *Successful Budgeting for Conferences and Seminars.* Manhattan, Kans.: Learning Resources Network (LERN), 1984.

Wagner, B. *Fee Management.* Manhattan, Kans.: Learning Resources Network (LERN), 1981.

Richard B. Fischer is associate director for program development and marketing with the Division of Continuing Education at the University of Delaware.

Once a list is used, its cost-effectiveness can be considered. Essentially, a list is cost-effective if it has "pulling power." This is determined by analysis that reflects the number of registrants or inquiries stemming from a purchased list. If a list "pulls" enough registrants on a continuing basis, then it is likely to be worth its cost. Unfortunately, it is usually not possible to ascertain cost-benefit information about a list in advance of its use.

Many schools grapple with the question of buying lists versus the alternative of building and maintaining their own lists. Since former registrants are the best prospects for subsequent offerings, it does make sense to try to build a list of former continuing education participants. For those on a list of degree credit students who have not registered in a given term (and who appear to be becoming "former customers"), an encouraging letter is sent, recommending a guidance appointment. A prepaid envelope is included to facilitate the return of a questionnaire in which students are asked about future registration intentions and for suggestions and observations about the programs of which they have been a part. This method encourages return of questionnaires and also provides insights into students' reasons for not registering.

Maintaining a list of persons who indicate interest in your offerings and who want to be placed on your mailing list can also be useful. East Carolina University's Division of Continuing Education attributes the continuing success of its annual "Tryon Palace Symposium" (a three-day program for decorative arts) to its careful cultivation and maintenance of a small but very high-quality mailing list. The list includes past participants in the symposium, friends of past participants, and members of antique, historical, and garden groups. In a given year, 75 percent of the registrants are past participants. The small size of the list and the importance of past participants permit a highly personalized letter to prospective clients, encouraging them to return. Conventional means of promotion are used to augment or replenish the basic list. Special attention is given to maintaining relationships with community groups whose interests are germane to the focus of the symposium.

Trying to capture and maintain other types of lists may not be useful or cost-effective. People move around so frequently that keeping any list up to date is difficult, even when computer systems are used. When computers are used to manage mailing lists, both processing and storage costs can become prohibitive if one maintains too many lists of marginal utility.

Combining purchased lists from whatever source—commercial list houses, community organizations, professional groups—with a limited number of locally maintained lists is an optimal approach for most organizations. Once again, the cost involved warrants careful attention.

In addition to managing mailing lists, there are other limitations to direct-mail advertising as a promotional tool. Principal among these is

Relating program location to the continuing education
agency's strategic plan is important for the unit's
marketing image and meeting student needs.

Locating Continuing Education Programs

Robert C. Mason

This chapter emphasizes the importance of program location as one component of a strategic plan that also considers the mission of the institution or agency, the marketing image desired, and needs of learners. It also discusses the relationships among program location and program quality, program costs, supportive services, and economies of scale.

Growing Importance of Effective Program Location

Although there is a substantial literature on participation in continuing education (Darkenwald and Merriam, 1982; Johnstone and Rivera, 1965), there is a paucity of literature directly concerning the location of programs, although location directly influences participation and is an area of concern for almost all continuing educators, regardless of their bases of operation.

When the location of continuing education programs is mentioned in the literature, it is usually tangential to other topics. Knowles (1970), for example, advocates providing good physical facilities congruent with the principles of andragogy and declares that locations of continuing education programs should "smell" adult. He notes that adults sometimes refuse to enroll in continuing education classes at public schools from

H. Beder (Ed.). *Marketing Continuing Education.*
New Directions for Continuing Education, no. 31. San Francisco: Jossey-Bass, Fall 1986.

which they have previously dropped out. Yet, when such programs are moved to sites with comfortable furnishings, such as abandoned warehouses, enrollment increases because these locations are different from places people have earlier learned to hate.

Kotler (1975) notes the need for organizations to be adaptive to environmental changes. In a situation of increasing competition and rapid social change, institutions and agencies must be ready to alter missions, goals, and strategies. Organizations must identify major strengths and weaknesses in all facets of continuing education, one of which is facilities and locations. Strategic planning and strategic management are vital tools for adapting locations and facilities to the major strengths of organizations.

Thinking Strategically About Locating
Continuing Education Programs

Kotler (1975) defines strategic planning as "a managerial process of developing and maintaining a strategic fit between the organization's goals and resources in its changing market opportunities" (p. 83). He uses the metaphor of "strategic window" for watching the changes within the environment and assessing the requirements for successful continuing education programming.

How does a continuing educator begin strategic planning with respect to program location? First, available resources must be identified and the capacity of the program assessed. Next, desired characteristics of off-campus locations must be identified in relation to what is available. Third, the needs and perceptions of off-campus students and faculty in existing programs should be assessed. Fourth, a formal plan to promote new locations among those who can influence location decisions, such as directors, presidents, deans, chairs, and faculty, needs to be devised and carried out; high-level support is required in large-scale location decisions.

By planning strategically, the continuing education unit becomes proactive rather than reactive and can obtain control over location decisions, rather than being told where to locate various educational programs.

When Education Becomes a Business

George Keller (1983) said, "The time has arrived for college and university leaders to pick up management's new tools and use them" (p. 118). Just as business is aware of and reacts to competition, so must continuing educators assess the strengths and weaknesses of their competition and program accordingly. For example, MBA courses should be placed where there are large concentrations of corporations, unless there are numerous similar programs already being offered by other reputable institutions. In the event of stiff competition, first determine if needs are already being met, and if they are, place your programs elsewhere.

A good business organization will monitor the current market very closely and ask fundamental questions. Are the courses that are currently being offered up to date? If the courses need computer support, are there computers available? The demographics of the area should be analyzed. Is the area a commuter town? If so, weekend classes or classes located on commuter trains might do well. If the average age is increasing in the area, perhaps courses on current issues—a very successful topic for older citizens—should be considered and located conveniently for the target audience. Trends that mandate integration of new skills or upgrading of skills should be noted. Teachers, for example, may need upgrading courses in math and science. In trend observation, be alert to the differences between trends and fads. Naisbitt (1984) notes that a fad begins at the top of our social structure, but a trend begins from the bottom and moves up.

Technology and Cooperative Ventures

With the introduction of electronic technology, the potential for cooperative programming with corporations is much greater. The electronic blackboard, telenet, and televideo, for example, allow programs to be provided at a number of locations while using the university as the transmittal site. This is very advantageous when a corporation or organization has a number of plants, building sites, or stations. Examples include school districts where there is a need for math and science upgrading, or major corporations where on-site bachelor's degree programs for employees might be appropriate.

Continuous Program Evaluation

Once a strategic plan has been developed, periodic evaluation needs to be conducted. Strategic planning should be ongoing, continuously considering the future while remaining in touch with the external world and its changing needs. Assessments should focus on program quality, cost-effective procedures, and student and faculty feedback and needs.

Marketing Image

Frequently, the location of continuing education programs receives less overall marketing effort than it deserves; the content, the presenter, the cost, and the target audience all receive greater priority. However, despite a significant investment in marketing, many programs have failed because of poor location choices. Strategically, locating a continuing education program in a plant, a school, or a hospital is generally an effective way to stimulate enrollments. Location is the key to success when programs are designed for military personnel, prison inmates, or professionals who desire to combine a vacation in a desired location with a continuing education activity.

The image, or symbolic value, of an off-campus location may be of major concern in some cases. For example, business college deans may become concerned when business courses are offered in high school settings, rather than in corporate conference rooms.

The choice of location should be related to specific goals of the continuing education unit. For example, the continuing education unit may desire to encourage external funding of educational activities by industry and may consider the location of continuing education programs in a corporate setting to be an important element in obtaining this goal. Some institutions and organizations are so concerned about this that they are willing to lose money on programs in order to increase the potential for external giving or funding.

Physical Presence

Harrington (1977) notes that it is desirable to have continuing education staff physically present at a site. He promotes the concept of learning centers, where there is someone always available who is competent to provide general information about both on-campus and off-campus programs. He suggests that a professional counselor is the ideal staff member, but a competent adult educator can perform the job effectively when trained to refer difficult questions to appropriate offices. A person with a demonstrated record of interpersonal skills is often the most effective in directing activities at a remote location. Harrington argues that off-campus adult credit students need this assistance, as they experience the same problems with registration, credit transfer, admission, and financial aid as their counterparts do on campus. Often, problems increase with distance from campus and uncertainty about various options available to adult learners. Most important, adult students are entitled to the same amenities afforded to main-campus students. If they cannot be on the main campus, then their need for study and break areas should be accommodated in a local or regional academic center.

Although enrollments can sometimes be temporarily increased by having numerous sites for classes, in the long run instructors and students prefer the stability and credibility of regional centers. Instructors and students alike prefer a year-round facility where they can interact with each other and become familiar with the locations of buildings, parking lots, classrooms, restrooms, and break rooms. Uncertainties in these areas become major problems when classes are moved frequently, and this can affect enrollments and the morale of off-campus faculty.

Enhancing Program Quality and Support Services

The centralization of as many learning options and services as possible at one location can enhance program quality and support services. Furthermore, with larger numbers of both credit and noncredit activities, it is easier to justify the presence of a professional continuing educator who can evaluate and help improve the programs offered. This staff person can also monitor student needs and desires and be available to answer questions from students and potential students, as well as from persons interested in special credit and noncredit activities. Program quality is also enhanced through the provision of computer labs, audiovisual equipment, and advisement. On-site continuing educators can arrange for periodic program advisement at central locations. Offering five to ten courses or other learning experiences per evening can promote collegiality among faculty and students alike, and coordinating class offerings and schedules makes it possible for students to enroll in several classes per week. The sheer volume of students in one location can justify such services as textbook sales, catalogue and course schedule distribution, and provision of application and registration information and promotional material for forthcoming activities.

If necessary, two or more institutions can collaborate to provide adequate resources, computers, audiovisual aids, and services necessary for high-quality programs. By working together, institutions and organizations can reduce overhead costs by sharing facilities and employees. Another tactic is to have advisers, counselors, and veteran assistance officers serve several off-campus centers by employing the "circuit rider" system, which has long been utilized by university extension service divisions.

Although organizing a large number of programs into centers can generally provide sufficient volume to justify support personnel, library reserve materials can still be a problem. Transporting materials to a nearby community college, private school, or college library may be the answer, because such libraries are generally open seven days a week and have longer hours than regional centers tend to maintain. For example, in Illinois, community colleges provide library services to upper-division university students taking classes within community college districts.

Grouping programs into centers can also facilitate much-needed research on the adult learner. On-site continuing educators can advertise this opportunity to various departments on the main campus and assist in the research effort, with the goal of improving adult instructional services.

Cost-Effectiveness

Just as centralizing many programs into a regional location can enhance program quality and support services, it also promotes cost-effectiveness. In a large county, as many as twenty univerity cars might be needed each evening for transporting faculty if classes were not centralized. By centralizing classes in one or two locations, only four to six cars are needed, because carpooling becomes feasible. Travel costs are thus reduced, and collegiality among faculty increases when they travel together. Northern Illinois University has formulated an effective carpooling arrangement, which reduced travel costs from $132,000 to $85,000 in one year's time. This reduction allowed teaching stipends to be increased for professors involved in off-campus instruction, thus making off-campus teaching more attractive. Grouping classes is advantageous in northern regions, where classes must sometimes be cancelled because of severe weather. In such circumstances, regional coordinators can initiate "telephone trees."

There are some disadvantages of concentrating classes in a few locations. In congested areas around large cities, ten to twelve miles may amount to thirty minutes of travel, and this can discourage students. Students generally like centers and the convenience they offer. They also appreciate the parking availability, the adult atmosphere, and the congeniality not always found on the main campus. Some students have appreciated off-campus centers enough to have contributed money to extension development funds to help provide more off-campus courses.

Factors to Consider in Selecting Locations

In the past, some agencies and organizations have provided free space to continuing education divisions offering off-campus courses. In areas around larger cities, where there are many agencies offering courses, there is often a charge, and this charge has increased as budgets have been cut and the demand for space has increased. Sometimes there is an advantage in a small charge, because leasing agencies are more cooperative in making the environment attractive to adult learners. It is important, for example, to have classrooms with tables instead of desks. Restrooms must be cleaned before evening classes. Lounges and vending machines should be available for breaks, and sometimes computer facilities are required. Apps (1981) indicates that having movable chairs is a minimum requirement for continuing education classrooms. Many institutions, especially universities, have started to charge an extra fee at off-campus sites to cover the cost of rent and special services. Most adult students are not reluctant to pay such a fee because of the services it allows.

Some adults enroll in courses to meet other people. Therefore, it is important to have an adequate number of break rooms, in addition to adequate security, safe sidewalks free from ice, and lighted parking lots and entrances.

Having students and instructors rate the quality of off-campus locations is an effective way to provide feedback for planning. Positive evaluations are useful in acquiring resources from the administration when there is need for improvement of the site.

Summary

Locating continuing education programs is important to all continuing educators, regardless of the organizations to which they are attached. It is important to relate program placement and desired marketing image to the mission and strategic plan of the organization.

Organizations that have some activity other than educating adults as their major function sometimes fail to adapt their programs to the unique needs of adults or to an ever-changing society and environment.

Although program location has generally been considered less important than content, presenter, and target audience, many programs have been cancelled because of inconvenient locations or failure to employ strategic planning in placing programs at particular sites.

Adult learners enrolled at remote locations need a comprehensive regional center, complete with resources comparable to those on the main campus. These resources should include an on-site director or coordinator, who can provide assistance with advisement, registration, admission, billing, textbook sales, library references, and so on.

Centralizing continuing education programs into a regional location can enhance accountability. Costs may be lowered as a result of carpooling or of sharing resources with other organizations associated with the learning center. Centralization of activities can result in increased opportunities for evaluation and research, student and faculty interaction, and a more positive image of the sponsoring organization. Faculty and student evaluations of continuing education locations and marketing efforts can assist with future planning and with the selection of new or the retention of current locations.

References

Apps, W. *The Adult Learner on Campus.* Chicago: Follett, 1981.

Darkenwald, G., and Merriam, S. *Adult Education: Foundations of Practice.* New York: Harper & Row, 1982.

Harrington, F. H. *The Future of Adult Education: New Responsibilities of Colleges and Universities.* San Francisco: Jossey-Bass, 1977.

Johnstone, J. W., and Rivera, R. J. *Volunteers for Learning.* Chicago: Aldine, 1965.

Keller, G. *Academic Strategy: The Management Revolution in Higher Education.* Baltimore: Johns Hopkins University Press, 1983.

Knowles, M. S. *The Modern Practice of Adult Education.* New York: Association Press, 1970.

Kotler, P. *Marketing for Non-Profit Organizations.* Englewood Cliffs, New Jersey: Prentice-Hall, 1975.

Naisbitt, J. *Megatrends.* New York: Warner Communications, 1984.

Robert C. Mason is a professor of adult and continuing education at Northern Illinois University and associate dean of the College of Continuing Education, where he directs the Research in Adult Continuing Education office. Previously he was faculty chair of the graduate program in adult continuing education.

*Continuing educators who operate in the free-market economy
are bound by ethical decision making and must reach for a
balance between educational values and marketplace goals.*

Ethical Issues in Marketing
and Continuing Education

Laurence D. Martel, Robert M. Colley

Why should there be a chapter on ethics in a book about marketing and
continuing education? After all, most continuing educators are decent individuals who generally attempt to do the right thing. Indeed, many people
consider that being ethical is what it means to be professional. Also, as
professionals, many continuing educators are members of such organizations as National University Continuing Education Association (NUCEA)
and Association for Continuing Higher Education (ACHE), which have
codes of ethics that are intended to guide professional conduct.

The Free Marketplace and Continuing Education

On further consideration, however, it may not be the professional
conduct of continuing educators that gives rise to ethical issues as they
relate to marketing. Rather, the ethical issues with which we are concerned
seem to surface when demands are made on the profession from within an
institution, or because of forces in the marketplace that impinge on the
profession, changing the nature of the duties and responsibilities one
might have. For example, when college presidents look to continuing
education to absorb dwindling traditional enrollments, the performance
quotas and productivity expectations for tuition revenues that result put

H. Beder (Ed.). *Marketing Continuing Education.*
New Directions for Continuing Education, no. 31. San Francisco: Jossey-Bass, Fall 1986.

continuing education in a situation in which conflicts between loyalties and obligations may arise. Presumably, as additional institutions enter the continuing education arena and as institutions widen their territorial scope to capture new markets, moral questions will emerge in terms of tactics of competition and delivery of quality services. Consequently, ethical or moral considerations arise with respect to marketing when continuing educators function as businessmen and women who conduct their activities in a free market in the attempt to solicit enrollments and, in many cases, to compete against other educational institutions for the same students.

When continuing education participates in the free-market economy and consequently engages in marketing and advertising, all the ordinary ethical considerations that apply to business people should be applicable to continuing educators. This creates a need to understand how the study of ethical issues can be a helpful tool.

For any business enterprise, the free marketplace is a world of aggressive competition, in which market forces sometimes dictate survival or demise. Since Adam Smith's *Wealth of Nations* first appeared in 1776, economic theory has generally held that the free pursuit of material self-interest by individuals, households, businesses, and institutions produces the optimum in economic equilibrium. This was the "invisible hand" of the market. Indeed, nineteenth-century economists equated the competitive market forces of supply and demand with Charles Darwin's biological forces of natural selection. Market competition was construed as a form of survival of the fittest. The lessons of the twentieth century have increased the role of government in the market, but the marketplace has remained basically competitive. For instance, we are all aware of the many small colleges that have been closed during the past decade, the decentralization of continuing education divisions within higher education, and the demand on continuing education to provide subsidy revenues to offset traditional enrollment decline. When survival, or the survival rhetoric, enters the sphere of decision making, working professionals must make business decisions in a context that also involves assessing their responsibilities and obligations to themselves, to their loved ones, to their co-workers, their employers, their professions, and society at large. There are good reasons why some of these "loyalties" would take precedence over others in certain situations, but decisions about what to do in circumstances of conflicting obligations are often agonizing to the conscientious person.

What Is an Ethical Issue?

It is precisely this difficulty—establishing one's obligations and resolving conflicts—that Socrates captured twenty-five hundred years ago, when he began the first systematic inquiry into what makes human life "good" and how we should act to do the right thing. These are questions of *ethics,* a term derived from the Greek term *ethos,* meaning permanent customs, whereas we inherit words like *morality* from the Latin *mores.* Both are used synonymously, to refer not to social manners and niceties but to fundamental, enduring, and universal principles that guide human action, such as telling the truth, fulfilling obligations, respecting the lives of others, avoiding deception, and so forth. Problems with establishing what one should do and how one should act regarding situations that involve these virtues are ethical issues. While some might confuse moral virtues with the social manners of a particular time and place, to behave ethically is generally to do the principled thing when to do otherwise would be contrary to being a morally good person.

When individuals engage in a professional activity, such as medicine, government, or continuing education, there is a compelling demand to engage in professional conduct—that is, to know what one is obliged to do and to do the right thing. But this is not always easy, because we do not always know what our obligations are, particularly when new demands are made on the profession. As we know, conflicts do arise, and it has been through many different efforts to develop systems of thought to help resolve moral conflicts that various ethical theories have evolved over the centuries. Thus, the study of ethics is in a genuine sense the study of conflict resolution through an assessment of one's beliefs, goals, role in the economy, and place in the society. However, the value of the study of ethics is not necessarily in solving problems, but rather in recognizing them for what they are and dealing with them in as rational a way as possible. The study of ethics provides a tool for identifying and clarifying the issues and can thereby help facilitate a reasonable framework for resolution. One of the weaknesses of codes of conduct is that they do not acknowledge that many ethical problems come to us in the form of dilemmas.

Two Approaches to Resolve Ethical Issues

Clearly, it is not enough to say, "Do the right thing" if we cannot determine in a particular situation of conflict just what the right thing is. Appealing to a code of ethics is not helpful, as mentioned earlier, because codes are too general and do not take account of complex situations, although sometimes they do have the benefit of raising people's consciousness. (The cynic might say that professional codes of ethics are mainly window dressing—self-serving public relations.) It is also clear that in making moral decisions in marketing, one cannot go by the prevailing social or professional standards (it was generally acceptable in the past to advertise to sell slaves.)

Historically, in an effort to resolve moral conflict, two general philosophical theories emerged about how to decide what is morally right or wrong or what one ought to do in given circumstances. These theories are intended to provide guidance that is more universal, beyond the ordinary tug and influence of day-to-day priorities, thus providing us with a general framework for moral decision making.

The two theories, which represent distinctly different approaches to ethical reasoning, are known as *deontology* and *teleology*. Deontological reasoning comes from the Greek word that means duty. What is essential for the deontologist is that all actions must be guided by universal rules or principles. The most famous practitioner of this approach was Immanuel Kant, an eighteenth-century German philosopher. Kant believed that the moral worth of an action lies in the act itself: A specific act is good or evil because it is done for the sake of what is right. Our reason will naturally guide us to act out of duty. This might sound obvious until we realize that deontological approaches to decision making do not generally take into account the consequences of any given act. From this perspective, acts are done for the sake of what is right, not because they will make someone happy or benefit a group in some way. The idea is to do what is right, not what one is inclined to do. Examples of duties we should think of as universally binding are, for Kant, telling the truth and keeping promises. Other deontological philosophers include these and other duties as prima facie guides to all conduct. They are inviolable, except under extreme circumstances, as in the case of lying to save the life of a loved one. The problem with deontological theories is that they might be said to focus on what is good and right but ignore the person.

We can see this principle working as a justification for institutions that establish unbending rules and regulations to carry out their missions. Institutions, such as colleges and universities, that regard themselves as having inherently worthwhile services tend to structure their services so that students are obliged to perform in certain regimented ways. Similarly, bureaucracies are also built on the principle that rational decisions will occur if one follows the rules and procedures. These systems justify their operations on the basis of duties and obligations to be carried out. However, does not common sense tell us that the consequences of acts are part of what we should think about when we assess moral behavior?

The second approach takes account of the consequences of action. The teleological view is that consequences, not duties, are the determining factors in deciding whether or not an act is moral. *Telos* is the Greek word for *end*. "Egoistic" theories take the position that if the consequences of an act are the best for you or your organization—that is, if they provide you with happiness (or success)—then they are justified. A modern version of the teleological approach is the utilitarian theory, which attempts to justify acts in terms of the greatest good for the greatest number. Expanding on egoism, this theory is most fully developed in the writings of John Stuart Mill, who believed that in the pursuit of happiness the largest number of people affected must be taken into consideration in determining the moral worth of an act. This extends self to society, and it extends a given institution to the general society it serves. So, in the case of a lie, if it had no foreseeable harmful consequences, it would not be an immoral act for a utilitarian. Also, a certain act might be justifiable, according to utilitarians, if most people benefited, even if the action viciously exploited a small number of people.

Philosophers certainly recognize that while such theories can be useful as guides to decision making, few real-world policy decisions are based on pure deontological or teleological grounds. Rather than choosing between these two incompatible approaches, perhaps we can transcend the dichotomy and arrive at a conceptual framework of moral decision making that will help us to be more careful about what we do in marketing and continuing education. Let us examine the marketing enterprise itself and the ethical issues that arise from it. As we proceed, we will consider both ethical approaches.

Ethical Issues in Marketing

As free enterprise has become more sophisticated, a shift has occurred in the area of marketing, from a sales mentality to a more comprehensive definition that includes several facets. These facets consist of analysis (determining what the consumer needs), production of the product or creation of a service according to that need, pricing of what is being sold, and advertising and promotion of the product or service. It is this final aspect of marketing that is usually foremost in people's minds when they think of abuses or moral problems in marketing, because it is at this stage when the producers of goods and services are in direct communication with the consumer. At this stage, a key argument in the ethics of marketing is whether advertising is inherently suspect in some way, perhaps manipulative or exploitative.

On one side of the argument, there are those critics who follow the John Kenneth Galbraith position that advertising is intrinsically unethical, since it is a function of the profit motive and merely a way for manufacturers or service organizations to convince the public to consume their goods and services—by manipulating public emotions, if need be. Of course, there are many cases of this sort of exploitation; two areas of obvious concern include subliminal advertising and advertising aimed at children. In both instances, the critics argue, the consumer is relatively defenseless; the producer has an unfair advantage and manipulates wants and desires.

Defending the other side of the debate are those who, like economist Paul Samuelson, maintain that advertising is inherently good—that it performs an invaluable role in the free-market economy. Without advertising, consumers could not make free and informed choices, since they would not have adequate information about the available options. Also favoring advertising is the economic position that, as products and services are advertised, competition is usually enhanced and prices decline, thus benefiting the consumer.

Some professionals seem to espouse a weaker version of Galbraith's position, since they feel that advertising is in some way unbecoming to their professions. In the past, continuing educators included themselves with doctors, lawyers, pharmacists, and others who snubbed advertising as unethical but who in fact did not wish to engage in advertising because it tends to induce price competition. Universities in general have often fallen into this category as well. Nevertheless, claiming that advertising is unbecoming simply does not meet the contemporary need for an acceptable justification for marketing and continuing education. The argument over whether marketing is inherently desirable seems to be more an issue of taste than an issue of ethics.

If professional groups are aware of the moral responsibilities that relate to their advertising practices, including those that affect colleagues as well as consumers, it does seem reasonable to believe that advertising can perform a useful social and business function and that persons who engage in advertising can be good citizens as well as good business people. Consequently, if we assume that advertising can be morally agreeable, under what conditions would it be acceptable to such professions as continuing education? There seem to be at least four conditions that require consideration: fraud, inadvertent deception, worth of product or service, and unfair competition.

First, and obviously, most of us would agree that fraudulent advertising is morally unacceptable. We have all heard horror stories about entrepreneurs chased from one state to another with their storefront colleges and phony degrees. In these instances, the consumer is at best misled into an expenditure he or she would otherwise not have made. At worst, misinformation about a product will lead to serious professional or psychological harm to the consumer, once the product or service is in use. Since fraud presupposes intent and harmful consequences, the utilitarian would find it morally unacceptable, and of course the deontologist would categorize fraud as a form of lying.

Continuing educators reading this volume are not apt to engage in outright fraud, but we must consider that fraud is a vague concept. While the most extreme cases come to mind, such as fictitious colleges and bogus correspondence programs, there is a continuum along which various actions and practices might be called fraudulent. There is a temptation, and perhaps an inclination, always to put the "best face" on programs in advertising and promoting them. Nevertheless, one must be on guard not to give in to the subtle kinds of omission or exaggeration that are actually forms of inadvertent deception. Does one, for example, put the campus's most imposing building on the cover of one's program brochure, even though there is no genuine connection between building and program?

While less obvious than blatant fraud, inadvertent deception is no less unacceptable. Even though it is more problematic, because it is unintentional, the moral quality of an act is not solely determined by motivation. How can one be responsible for unintentionally deceiving people who will interpret the advertisements they read according to their own views? Consider an example from a *Wall Street Journal* advertisement for an international program, which gave a minimum score on the TOEFL examination for admission to the program. One applicant took that advertisement to mean that if she had at least that score, she was guaranteed admission. The crucial questions here concern how much responsibility the producer must take to avoid all possible misunderstanding and how much responsibility must rest on the shoulders of the consumer.

In response to the question of who bears the responsibility for inadvertent deception, the federal courts seem to be favoring the consumer by moving gradually toward the position of caveat vendor—let the provider of services and products beware. Of course, moral considerations reach far beyond legal issues. For a morally responsible user of advertising, it should not be just a matter of what one can get away with in a legal sense. The problem of inadvertent deception is complex and requires the serious attention of anyone who engages in the advertising aspects of marketing.

If you or one of your colleagues, for instance, publish that your program's faculty-student ratio is one to ten, do you ignore that for the past four semesters the course has enrolled thirty-five students? If it is advertised that a person can get a university degree through the evening division, is it implied that all degree programs are accessible during the evening? The temptation to lapse into certain kinds of deceptive claims is strong, as competition in the marketplace increases. Do the graduates of your programs really find jobs on a regular basis, as your catalogue implies? Does your certificate program really lead to wonderful careers in the computer industry? Is the sort of omission or deception suggested in these examples justifiable?

From the deontologist's perspective, these could be cases of misrepresentation, and absolute truth should be presented at all times, even if some undesirable consequences take place. Also, the idea of deception is inherently degrading to the deceiver, as well as to the deceived, creating an atmosphere of con-artistry. One's integrity is jeopardized in these instances.

In contrast, the utilitarian would view the use of omission and promotional exaggeration from the perspective of the results. As we have seen above, this could take different forms, depending on the type of utilitarian view. Thus, an egoistic utilitarian would say that the greatest good—for him alone or for the institution he represents—would be the overriding factor. This view can be extended to the idea that the most important loyalty is to the firm. The greatest good for the college or university should be the determining factor. This is a version of the "bottom line" mentality. The universalistic utilitarian would look beyond personal or institutional benefit and consider the overall value to the greatest number of consumers as the major principle for determining the moral worth of a policy or an action.

However, given even the most universalistic utilitarian approach, the fact that a few are misled might be acceptable—the cost of doing business, as it were. Time and cost are obvious factors with which to be reckoned. One cannot spend unlimited time and money attempting to avert all possible misreadings or qualify every generalization in the interests of the "whole truth."

These, of course, are matters of focus and degree, but one might be convinced that successfully promoting a program requires exaggeration or omission. According to this position, it is one's duty to promote and entice people who would not ordinarily or freely choose to participate in programs that can benefit them. In these instances, the consequences to the educator, the institution, and the consumer can be weighed; although deception is inherently undesirable, its undesirabiliity can be overridden if certain beneficial consequences so dictate. Although flexible, this view is dangerous in that it opens up the possibility of doing harm by compromising the institution and individual consumers, on the basis of other people's decisions about what can be delivered.

This leads to the third consideration: the worth of a product or a service. There are deeper questions that all of those who advertise must ask. Is the product or service inherently worthwhile or socially beneficial? One can tell the truth about a product, but if the product is socially harmful, then promoting it is immoral, at least on the face of it. For example, if racism and sexism are immoral, advertising that promotes exclusion based on race or sex is immoral. Extending the concept of worth, as it relates to an institution's mission, one could ask if some activities are appropriate within the domain of responsibility. Of course, one could argue that a college or university has no domain—that anything having anything to do with human inquiry, learning, or training is the business of continuing education. However, this view might reach beyond an institution's mission.

Nevertheless, continuing educators often justify anything in the name of education or generating revenues. There are the examples of certificate programs in belly dancing. There may be a need to train sanitation workers in vector-borne disease control, but is that sort of activity compatible with the role of a college or university? Does one chase the flow of dollars? Consider the plethora of programs that have come and gone as public policy has shifted the flow of funds for training. We are reminded of the minister who chased ambulances to make sure that if people died, he would be on hand to collect the funeral fees.

The point is that one must consider actions and activities in terms of their inherent moral value. We have a fairly good idea of how the deontologist would react: "Know what your duty is and carry on, conducting yourself and representing your institution in activities of inherent worth." Of course, when two oughts conflict—for example, promoting the fiscal health of the institution versus optimizing student services—there must be a rank-ordering of prima facie duties, and not all deontologists would agree on the ranking. The teleologist would probably require you to weigh your decisions according to their value to the people to whom you deliver services. If belly dancing leads to greater health, then you are obliged to fulfill that need, regardless of your charter, unless in the long run you do harm to your own institution. One must resolve the issue of inherent worth satisfactorily, as one positions oneself in the marketplace.

Turning to the fourth condition, unfair competition can be viewed as a form of deception, since techniques to gain advantage over a competitor are usually involved. This, of course, might include either making promises or implying benefits that are not verifiable. Offering inducements, such as financial aid, discounted tuition, or contract rates, can sometimes be construed as waging a price war, yet if one assumes a free marketplace, all sorts of behavior can be justified under the rationalization "That's business."

The free hand of ingenuity, creativity, and resourcefulness sometimes seems to take precedence over professional collegiality or common protocol. For example, if a new continuing education division wishes to begin business by entering the established market of another traditional continuing education college, to compete for the same students by creating similar programs, is one obliged to follow any rules of conduct? Indeed, are there any rules, including common decency? Is there a territorial or regional propriety or an obligation not to invade or steal another's specialty?

A related example involves collusion in competition. For instance, is it fair for a non-profit college to join with a proprietary school to capture a market served by community colleges? To what degree does collegial cooperation count as restraint of trade in the free-market economy, resulting in controls over the marketplace? Is college and university nonprofit status jeopardized by continuing education practices that compete with proprietary institutions and trade schools?

As with cases of fraud, unfair competition is not easy to identify, beyond the classic stone-throwing tactics. When it does surface, moral injury is often a matter of interpretation. Again, the deontologist would say, "It is your obligation to tell the truth, not to cheat or mislead people." The teleologist would want to determine moral culpability by the outcomes.

Summary and Recommendations

It is clear that the circumstances surrounding acceptable advertising involve complex moral considerations, which are not easily understood by appeals to either traditional approaches or ethical issues. How, then, should the continuing education professional proceed? Should one take the deontological approach and determine the duties and obligations of the profession and establish a marketing strategy in accordance with those principles? Or, should one take the teleological approach and determine all marketing plans and actions in accordance with a justification of the greatest good to the numbers served, including the health of the continuing education unit? Maybe you do not wish to lie, but how much truth are you obligated to reveal in your marketing? Perhaps you should question if, indeed, you should survive.

One can understand that these two approaches are in opposition, and that either by itself is probably inadequate for making ethical decisions about marketing or any other area of human activity. The danger of the teleological approah is that it tends to focus on the aggregate benefits and ignore potential harm to the individual. The danger of the deontological approach is that it relies on duty and obligation and disregards potential consequences. However, we are not reduced to choosing between an ethics of happiness and ethics of duty. These approaches can be helpful in the process of ethical problem solving, if one is aware of both views and the dichotomies they create.

To have these intellectual tools at hand better equips us to do the sort of analysis of circumstances and values that leads to acceptable actions. This is not easy, particularly since values are not facts. Indeed, values are the kinds of ideals toward which we strive. Even though they are never completely attainable, values thirst for continual realization. For example, one might fall short of the mark by misleading someone today but rectify the situation and try to advertise less ambiguously in the future.

For continuing educators, perhaps combining an articulation of the values of continuing education as not only an extension of the educational system but also a profession may be a useful framework for measuring one's activity as often as one evaluates the general ledger. A format for such an effort could include reading volumes like this one, attending association conferences and regional meetings, and simply thinking about potential ethical problems before they arise.

For our purposes, we are not speaking of extreme cases of villainy, although there are plenty of those. We are addressing decent people who think that when "push comes to shove," certain forms of deception, such as omission, are justified by the free-market economy or by loyalty to the firm. Deception has also been rationalized on the grounds that it is extremely time-consuming or prohibitively expensive to market in the most ethical way or even to correct an ethical problem once it has been discovered.

Clearly, it is self defeating to be immobilized by an overdeveloped sense of duty. Given tradition and the inherent worth of one's programs, one should consider the consequences of what one does in relation to educational needs and resources in the community. There is almost a moral imperative to change to fit needs, on utilitarian grounds, and to continuously verify what you say you are doing. Nevertheless, the forward-thinking marketer must be cautious and consider the deontological position that there is an obligation to protect the integrity and quality of the institution, as well as one's own integrity. In the best Aristotelian sense, one must reach for a balance, a golden mean between a policy that maximizes educational goals and one that enhances marketplace goals. There is also the tension between what one, as a continuing educator, might wish to do if circumstances permitted and what one is strictly obligated to do, in the deontological sense. Such conflicts generally require a compromise of values. This would include such things as funding unprofitable programs for the disadvantaged from profits generated by popular but only peripherally educational courses.

If one thing is clear about the issue of ethics and marketing continuing education, it is that the decision-making process is filled with problems, with no quick-fix solutions. Yet within the quagmire of moral conflict, the study of ethics can be a very useful tool in evaluating and selecting one's own rational and systematic approach.

Laurence D. Martel is the director of the Office of Opportunity Education and Research at University College, Syracuse University. He also teaches professional ethics in the College of Human Development.

Robert M. Colley, director of Independent Study Degree Programs and the IBM School of Independent Contract Programs for Syracuse University's University College, also teaches business ethics for the Syracuse University School of Management.

The essential tools for programs' success must be placed within the appropriate strategy.

Summary

Hal Beder

If there has been one consistent theme in this sourcebook, it is that marketing is far more than slick program promotion. Rather, marketing is a comprehensive strategy for inducing learners to exchange resources they value—time and money, for example—for something they value more: education. As each author has suggested in one fashion or another, for the strategy to be successful, three conditions must be met. First, the marketing orientation must pervade all aspects and all levels of programming, from the operation of individual learning activities to the management of the entire continuing education unit. Second, marketing must proceed from the goals of the larger institution, and marketing plans must have the support of one's superiors. If this principle is ignored, continuing educators soon find themselves in conflict with their sponsoring institutions. Third, marketing is a strategic activity and, as such, requires constant planning and continuous assessment.

As Smith notes in the second chapter, the marketing process begins with an assessment of institutional goals, available resources, the nature of the competition, and the needs and preferences of learners. On the basis of this initial assessment, the audience is segmented into groups, according to how each group is expected to respond to blends of program, promotion, price, and location.

Once markets have been thus defined, consideration must be devoted to the programs, or "product," to be delivered to market segments

H. Beder (Ed.). *Marketing Continuing Education.*
New Directions for Continuing Education, no. 31. San Francisco: Jossey-Bass, Fall 1986.

selected for service. Willard and Warren aptly note that product decisions must be considered holistically and recommend the use of a market grid to facilitate this process. They further note that development of new products for new markets entails substantial risk. Generally speaking, it is wiser to concentrate on achieving a larger share of current markets or to probe new markets with modest adaptations of currently successful programs. Fads and blind entry into new markets because they seem "hot" are inconsistent with the strategic approach to marketing. Although promotion, price, and location are important factors, in the long run the quality of programs is the most important ingredient in achieving success.

Yet for learners to participate in programs, they must be aware of them. This requires communication, the role of promotion. Falk explains that promotion must be planned with respect to such factors as cost, potential learners' preferences for messages and media, and the amount of promotion required to meet enrollment goals. There are the four responses that should be gained from promotion embodied in the AIDA principle: A, getting attention; I, stimulating interest; D, creating desire; and A, prompting action. Promotional messages should be designed to elicit all AIDA responses. Falk goes on to discuss the strengths and weaknesses of various promotional media, including newspapers, magazine advertising, radio and television, direct mail, telemarketing, and personal contact. Personal contact, he notes, is a particularly powerful method that is often overlooked.

Pricing, writes Fischer, begins with various pricing objectives: to break even, recover out-of-pocket costs only, recover all costs, make a profit, or even lose money (as in some community service programs). Pricing requires knowledge of various costs. Direct costs are those directly attributable to the program; indirect costs, or overhead, pertain to the general operation of the unit and are difficult to ascribe to a particular program. Sunk costs are those that a program incurs even if it is cancelled.

In establishing price, programs need to know how much the program costs, how much of a fee the participants are likely to pay, and how many participants are likely to enroll. Pricing, far from being the mere manipulation of a formula, requires judgment. For example, if the program is large enough to yield sizable income or has no promotional costs, or if there is very little risk involved, price might be reduced. However, if participants' fees are paid by third parties or if an affluent or profit-making group is being served, then initial price estimates may be increased.

Price, aside from its obvious economic relationship to participation, also has symbolic meaning. Price is significantly related to perceptions of quality. Continuing education units must consider this in projecting images of prestige, bargain-basement service, or a midpoint.

Program location is an important ingredient in the marketing strategy, for at least two reasons. First, the location of a program determines its accessibility and, obviously, accessibility is an important factor in learner participation. Second, locations have symbolic value, and the image conveyed by the location is projected onto the program itself. As Mason notes in his discussion of location, the image conveyed by a high school location may be inappropriate to a program designed for corporate executives. Mason goes on to strongly advocate the regional learning center approach, whereby many educational activities are conducted at centralized sites. Learning centers reduce costs and enable the provision of supportive services that are difficult to provide when sites are widely scattered.

Marketing, of course, is subject to abuse. Therefore, ethical issues must be considered in developing marketing strategies. As Martel and Coley explain, most potential abuses stem from the economic, or "marketplace," orientation of marketing, which tends to emphasize maximization of income and learner participation. Two central questions arise from concerns for truth in advertising and program focus. With respect to program focus, for example, should continuing educators focus on socially important programming that benefits those in greatest need, regardless of their ability to pay? Or should we focus on programs of high learner demand for more affluent audiences, the kinds of programs that produce the greatest participation and income? Although these two options are not always incompatible, they frequently are.

In making value decisions, continuing educators must balance two approaches to ethics. One approach, deontology, focuses on absolute duty. According to this approach, such things as lying and breaking promises are always wrong. The other approach, teleology, stresses the relative nature of ethics: The consequences of an act are what is most important, and who benefits becomes the moral test.

In conclusion, marketing is an overarching programming strategy based on sound theory and tested in practice. As many continuing education units have found, application of marketing principles can lead to program success. Yet, as with all program planning systems, success is contingent on deliberate action and constant re-evaluation according to the goals of the organization.

Hal Beder is associate professor of adult and continuing education at Rutgers University.

Index

A

ACORN (A Classification of Residential Neighborhoods), 25
Advertising: concept of, 13; ethics of, 95-96
Advisory board, for pilot testing, 40, 42-43
AIDA principle, in promotion, 50, 60, 104
Alabama in Birmingham, University of, telemarketing by, 64-65
Anderson, R. E., 74, 81
Ansoff, I. H., 11, 17
Apps, W., 88, 89
Aristotle, 101
Assessment: of competition, 21-22, 38; of needs, wants, and demands, 11; of programs, 30
Association for Continuing Higher Education (ACHE), 91
Atmospherics, concept of, 13

B

Bentley College, test-piloting by, 40, 43
Beder, H., 1, 3, 17, 105
Benefits, essential, and value, 5-6
Booz, Allen, and Hamilton, 47*n*
Brigham Young University, direct mail by, 61

C

California at San Diego, University of, promotion planning at, 53
Cluster analysis, and geographic segmentation, 25
Colley, R. M., 1, 91, 101, 105
Collins, K. S., 60, 71
Competition: and market, 21-22, 38; unfair, ethical issues of, 99
Competition-oriented pricing, concept of, 16
Computer technology, for marketing, 27

Concentrated marketing, and segmentation, 7
Consumer analysis, principles of, 9-11
Continuing education: as business, 84-85; changes in, 1; defining and analyzing market for, 19-28; ethical issues in, 91-101; and free marketplace, 91-92; place for, 83-90; pricing for, 73-81; program development in, 29-48; promotion for, 49-71
Contract pricing, as option, 80
Cooperation, and technology, 85
Core product, and marketing, 5, 12-13
Cost-effectiveness: and place, 88; and promotion, 68
Cost-oriented pricing, concept of, 15-16
Costs: direct or indirect, 75; fixed or variable, 75-76; levels of, 74-75; percentage of, 78-79; sunk or risk, 76; and value, 6
Cross, K. P., 23, 28

D

Darkenwald, G., 83, 89
Darwin, C., 92
Deception, inadvertant, ethical issues of, 97-98
Demand-oriented pricing, concept of, 16
Demands: assessing, 9-11; states of, 10
Demographic segmentation, variables in, 7, 23-24
Deontology, as approach to ethics, 94, 96, 97, 99, 100
Development, of product, 12
Differentiated marketing, and segmentation, 7-8
Direct mail, for promotion, 56, 60-63
Discounting, as pricing option, 79-80
Diversification, of product, 12

E

East Carolina University, mailing list of, 62

107